HANS G. ISENBERG

GREAT
RACING
CARS
OF THE WORLD

CHARTWELL
BOOKS, INC.

Michael Schumacher (Benetton Ford) has gone straight to the top in Grand Prix racing (below). He wows the fans with his clever driving just as much as the sponsors, who want to make the young man from Kerpen into a media star. A career in Formula 1 is more than ever a really tough job; unfair regulations and dishonest practices make life difficult for all concerned. Front–engined racers then and now: the red 250F Maseratis (right) and the 800 bhp American "Outlaws" (far right) provide motor racing in its purest form. Truck racing is rather more basic in style (center). The American specialists in the technique of drifting spend more time going sideways than straight

CONTENTS

RISKY BUSINESS

A Maserati 250F (on the left) and an Alfa Romeo 158, or "Alfetta", at the start of a historic race. Fangio won the Argentinian GP in 1954 in a Maserati 250F, and in 1957 he drove one to win his fifth and last Drivers' World Championship. It had 260 bhp from 2,493 cc, 6 cylinders unblown, maximum 172 mph (275 kph). The "Alfetta" won ten Grands Prix between 1947 and 1951; supercharged straight eight engine giving 380 bhp from 1,479 cc and 181 mph (290 kph)

Frank Williams' British
team only became one of
the top teams of
Formula 1 in 1975,
scoring four wins with
Keke Rosberg and Nigel
Mansell. They were using
the still rather unreliable
turbocharged Honda V6
RA 163E with a capacity
of 1,477 cc and 900 bhp
at 11,400 rpm. Mansell
showed he had class

With three world championship titles to its credit, the 1.5 liter TAG-Porsche turbocharged V6 engine was the most successful power unit of the turbo era. It gave 850 bhp at 11,000 rpm but only weighed 330 pounds (150 kg), had two KKK turbos blowing at 2.6 bar, and was installed in the McLaren carbon fiber chassis.

Drivers who step into another's shoes usually find it difficult. In 1983 Patrick Tambay was supposed to perform the same heroic deeds for Ferrari as Gilles Villeneuve, who had been killed in an accident. The comparison with Villeneuve was bound to be unfavorable; Gilles had been the team's favorite and an unremitting fighter, while Tambay was a gentleman driver.

THE HEROIC AGE OF THE FIRST RACES

Karl Benz and Gottlieb Daimler produced their first "racers" in 1899. 10 bhp was enough for victory

This white Mercedes racing car of 1906 was capable of over 90 mph (150 kph). Wilhelm Maybach designed the 11,984 cc 6 cylinder engine which gave 125 bhp. Emil Jellinek (far right), held to have been the first owner of a racing team, also had the idea to use the name Mercedes for the marque. His energies were equally divided between diplomacy, fast cars and beautiful women. He also sold the newfangled bicycles to the affluent clientele of the Côte d'Azur

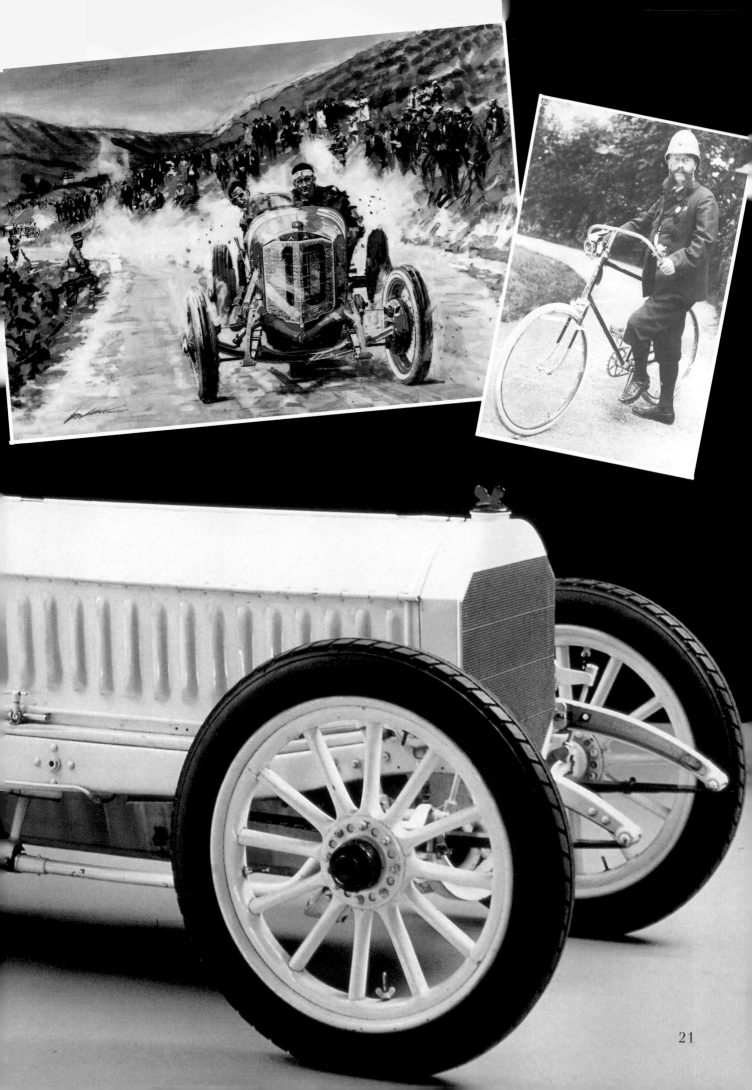

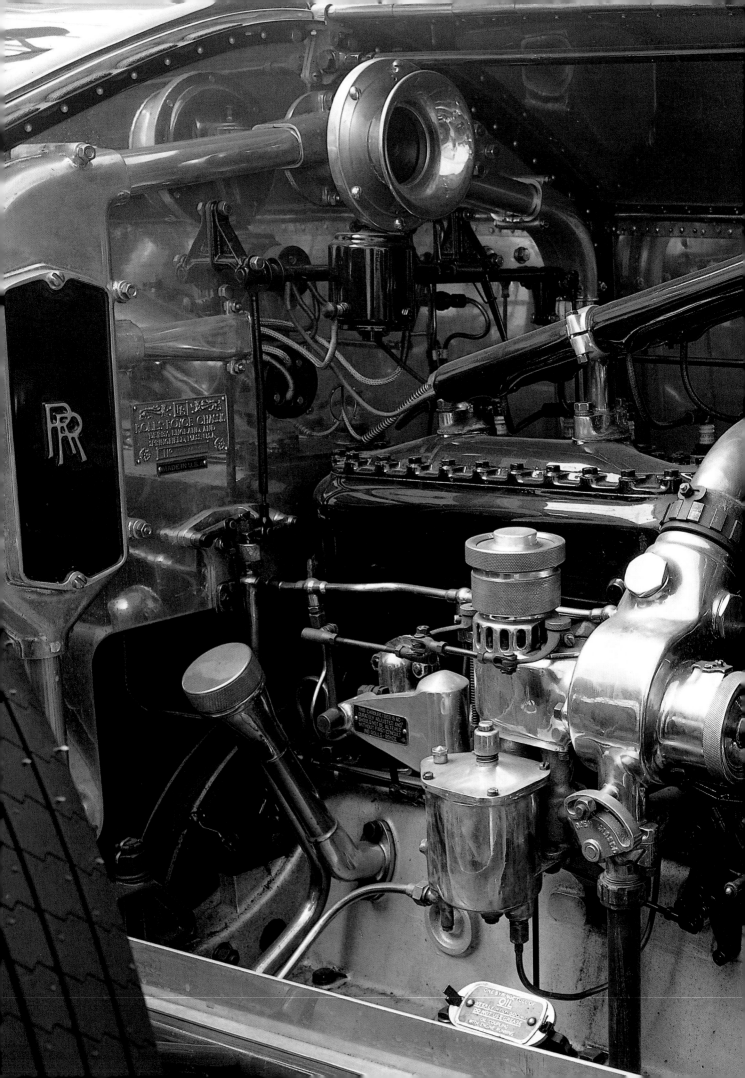

This Rolls–Royce Silver Ghost engine was built under license at the Springfield works in the USA. Its wealthy owner felt he could not trust the U.S. racing cars to perform reliably. In many a long distance race its faster rivals fell out, and the Rolls–Royce won. Unlike the standard British model, this U.S. version of the 7,428 cc straight six engine had twin coil ignition and no magneto. The owner quotes its output as 135 bhp

Few other racing cars were so far ahead of their time as Ettore Bugatti's Type 35 (right). Between 1924 and 1930 the 2 liter and later 2.3 liter eight cylinder racer won more than 200 races, including the 1926 French Grand Prix, against the best racing cars of the day. Bugatti also created a 1.5 liter version of the supercharged straight eight engine and (for Peugeot) a 1,000 cc four cylinder engine using half a Type 35 block

The British Rileys were often entered in competition. Before the Second World War Rileys were often seen at the famous Brooklands Motor Course, where they did very well especially in the 1100 cc class. Famous designers Reid Railton and Parry Thomas worked there on this very low–built sports racer, which was in fact called the Brooklands. Its greatest success was the outright win in the 1932 Tourist Trophy race

In 1926 the 1.5 liter NSU racing cars (left) had a sensational 1–2–3–4 class win in the German Grand Prix at the Nürburgring. Their success was due to a six cylinder engine with a permanently engaged Roots blower

A radically new design can only prove its worth in motor sport after much development. The Tropfenwagen ("teardrop cars") designed in 1923 by Edmund Rumpler for Benz (right and foot of page) were the first mid–engined racing cars, capable of 112 mph (180 kph)

No other small car manufacturer scored so many successes before the Second World War as Morgan. The Super Sports three–wheeler with its JAP engine could easily reach 90 mph (145 kph). In record attempts at Brooklands in 1926 a racing Morgan even recorded 119 mph (190 kph)

SENSATION IN 1923: MID ENGINE AND INBOARD BRAKES

It is July 7, 1908, at the French Grand Prix for automobiles in Dieppe. The Berlin journalist Walter Oertel wires the following report to the offices of the periodical *Motorwagen:* "Eyewitnesses say that the car began to sway on the straightaway between Cziel and Eu when traveling at a tremendous speed, whether as a result of tire failure or a steering fault will never be known. It then skidded to the left and flew over the ditch at the side of the road, uprooting two trees, and rolled over twice. Cissac had his chest crushed by the steering column and lived for a few minutes, while his mechanic Staub's skull was smashed."

And yet the history of motor racing had started harmlessly enough. Ten years after the invention of the automobile this revolutionary development was going through a period of crisis. Hardly anyone in their senses would have anything to do with these noisy, smelly and extremely temperamental vehicles. The electric car manufacturers' lobby attacked the supporters of the steam cars, while the aficionados of the gasoline engine were branded as reckless daredevils. What was needed was some good publicity. The French had the right idea, and invited all the important automobile firms to come to Paris to take part in a competition that was to be as fair as possible. Daimler and Benz among others did not let the opportunity slip. The start of the world's first motor race was on June 11, 1895, in Versailles near Paris. In addition to the six steam cars and 14 gasoline–engined vehicles, a fast electric automobile was there to excite the enthusiastic populace. It is most unlikely that the simple country folk had ever seen one of these strangely whirring machines before. Nine cars reached the finish in Versailles at the end of the 500 mile (800 km) marathon to Bordeaux

The chief designer at Daimler–Benz, Ferdinand Porsche (above), went from success to success in building racing cars between 1923 and the end of 1928. He achieved maximum power with the aid of supercharging. But it was only in 1936 at Auto Union that he was able to realize his concept of a mid–engined 16 cylinder racer. Above right: the Barnato Hassan, a Brooklands special with 8 liter Bentley engine

The Grand Prix race as a social event (above).

Ralph de Palma was born to stardom. The Mercedes driver even changed his tie before the Indianapolis 500; he never started a race without it

and back. There were several deaths and many injuries. The efficiency of the Daimler principle was clearly demonstrated, as the first six finishers were gasoline–engined. The fast steamers failed because of the thirst of their boilers, which had to be filled up with 30 liters of water every 30 miles (50 km). This cost more time than the same operation with the gasoline–engined vehicles which boiled away about 10 liters of coolant on average every 60 miles (100 km). The cooling fan was not introduced until 15 years later.

But to return to the legendary French Grand Prix of 1908, which was run over a distance of 478 miles (770 km). At half distance the French Benz works driver, Hémery, was up among the leaders. When overtaking another competitor his goggles were shattered by a stone. Our reporter from Berlin takes up the story: "The splinters of glass entered his eye. Maddened by the sudden violent pain, Hémery let go of the steering wheel and tried to clutch his eye with both hands. Had not the car happened to be on a straight, smooth stretch of road, an accident would have been inevitable. Hémery grasped the steering wheel again and completed the lap. Back at his pit, he had the glass splinters removed from his eye by a doctor who had been quickly called, climbed back into his car and completed the race."

On the penultimate lap all hell was let loose in the pits. All the available tires had been used up, although André Michelin had supplied 1,200. Our reporter reckoned one of the reasons for this was the daredevil driving of the Italian Fiat works drivers and the French: "The professional Italian drivers throw their cars into the corners and make them skid round at the rear. This driving method naturally places an enormous sideways

31

600 BHP AND 210 MPH (338 KPH): REALLY HARD WORK AT THE WHEEL

Even for drivers with many years, racing experience, the Mercedes W125 of 1937 was a staggering experience (large picture). The tremendous torque of the straight eight engine of 5660 cc came in with a bang when the blower was engaged. Only a few drivers were able to get the best out of this car over the full Grand Prix distance of 312 miles (500 km). Hermann Lang (right) came second in the 1937 Italian Grand Prix behind Rudolf Caracciola (left), and so had oil, dust and rubber thrown into his face. In 1938 Mercedes came in 1–2–3 in the Tripoli Grand Prix (above). Hans Stuck (above right), the "diplomat in racing overalls".

pressure on the inside front wheel, and it is only too likely that the detachable rim will come away with such rough treatment." The power slide had been born. After 6 hours 55 minutes our man on the spot reports one last time from the circuit: "From the stir on the stands one can tell that a car is approaching. And now one can hear the Mercedes engine. The brightly glittering Mercedes shoots along the straightaway, greeted by thunderous applause from the Germans present and cheers from the French." Christian Lautenschlager's average speed for the 478 miles (770 km) over unmade roads was an amazing 69.042 mph (111.107 kph) in spite of 12 tire changes and stops for fuel and water. For 6 hours 55 minutes the fastest of the Mercedes works drivers had been working very hard indeed. His top speed had been an astonishing 112 mph (180kph). The injured Hémery was six minutes behind and still took second place in his Benz. Summing up this exciting race, the reporter of *Motorwagen* says: "It is absolutely certain that the French automobile industry, whose national pride has been deeply hurt after being toppled from the dizzy heights of success, will make the utmost efforts to avenge this humiliating defeat. There is a hard fight in store for us, much harder than it was this year." Our reporter was wrong. The First World War was soon to start. In place of the sporting rivalry on the racing circuits there would be the bitter earnest of the battlefields. There was no racing until 1918. The Indianapolis 500 Mile Race in 1919 was the first race with a first class field supported by the works. Howdy Wilcox won on a four cylinder Peugeot; it was to be the last victory there by a European car for another 20 years.

AFTER THE WAR: RED IN THE ASCENDANT

Rivals hadn't a chance against the Alfa Romeo racers. The "Alfetta" could win at will

After the Second World War, Italian cars dominated the scene (and not only with the noise they made). The French Talbot Lagos and Gordinis and the British ERAs only had any real chance of victory in the hands of private entrants in their various national races. On the Grand Prix circuits the Alfa Romeo 158s and Maserati 4CLTs outperformed them, as did later the Lancia D50 (seen here with Alberto Ascari at the wheel) and Maserati 250F (large picture). The brilliantly designed engine of the Alfa Romeo 158/9 or "Alfetta" (far right) gave up to 400 bhp from only 1,479 cc

A comparison between the prewar Mercedes W125 and the Ferrari 375 of 1951 shows that the postwar racer is more compact. Ferrari and Maserati were always playing second fiddle to the unbeatable Alfettas, until Ferrari came out with the 380 bhp unblown 4,498 cc V12, which beat the Alfa Romeos in the 1951 British Grand Prix

Veritas Meteor 2 liter 6 cylinder racing engine. From 1948 to 1953 Ernst Loof was responsible for the fastest German racing cars of the immediate postwar period. This fine in–line engine was based on the BMW 328. The Heinkel aero engine factory helped him to find more power. Mathé's four cylinder Porsche single seater was a great rarity (below). In the early postwar years speedway racing was very popular

16. Internationales
ADAC·EIFEL·RENNEN
31. Mai 1953 8 Uhr
NÜRBURGRING

For nearly 20 years the Indianapolis racers could also take part in Grand Prix races, so the fastest of them ran in the Italian Grand Prix at Monza in the 50s. The Indianapolis 500 therefore counted for the World Championship. The A type Connaught (main picture) was a British contender for Formula 2 honors. The later B type achieved fame by beating the Italians in the hands of Tony Brooks, winning the 1955 Syracuse Grand Prix

Paul Russo entered the 1946 Indy race in this car with one Offenhauser engine at the front and another at the back. Second fastest in practice, he had an accident on the 16th lap

Billy de Vore drove the six-wheeled Kurtis Offenhauser into 12th place in the 1948 Indy 500. For 17 laps he had been in front

Sam Hanks built a V16 out of two straight eight Miller engines, and used four-wheel drive. He broke the lap record in practice

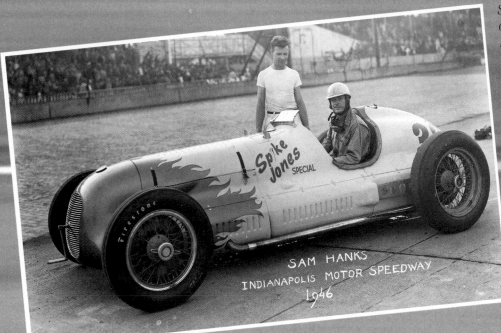

In 1954 there were no such things as roll bars and safety belts, so Keith Hall (who had been almost certain of victory) was thrown out of his Cooper–Bristol when he had a spin. He got off with spinal injuries. Emergency services at the Nürburgring in 1955 (right). Original caption: "The fire was put out with consummate ease."

TALENT SPOTTER JOHN COOPER AND HIS MINI RACERS

In every era of racing there were outstanding drivers and race managers. And yet the stars of the thirties were a race apart. Rudolf Caracciola, Bernd Rosemeyer and the Mercedes team manager Alfred Neubauer are still names to conjure with, although the days of their greatest successes and failures are more than 55 years ago.

After the First World War, the European Grand Prix races were clearly dominated by the French, British, and Italian private entrants. In America Indianapolis was a great draw with all its blaze of publicity. The Mercedes team which had been so successful before the First World War decided to confront the American Indianapolis specialists in 1923, their first postwar race on foreign soil. Back in 1915 Ralph de Palma had had a surprise win in the 500 Mile Race in a Mercedes. It was hoped that the new supercharged 4 cylinder cars would be able to wipe the floor with the American Miller and Duesenberg 8 cylinder racers. Ettore Bugatti had the same idea, because the American market could best be won by means of a spectacular victory in the Indianapolis 500. The development of the supercharger was based on an invention made by the Swiss Arnold Zoller, who worked to improve the performance of aero engines in the First World War. The supercharger forces the air and fuel mixture into the combustion chamber with excess pressure. Paul Daimler, son of the founder of the firm, designed the first supercharged Mercedes racer for the Indianapolis race.

The description of the German drivers in the American press was hardly flattering: "fat–bellied German brewers and butchers." Their size had its advantages. In most European races, all repairs had to be carried out using only tools and materials carried on the car. Numerous tire

The British method of training young drivers: "Since British roads almost always end in a roundabout, drivers learn the four–wheel drift almost automatically," remarked ex–world champion Jackie Stewart. In fact no other country has had so many great drivers since the war. Many of them had their first taste of racing in the tiny 500 cc racers, such as the mid-engined Coopers. The pretty Formula Junior Elva (above) was ideally suited to the needs of the beginner in the 60s

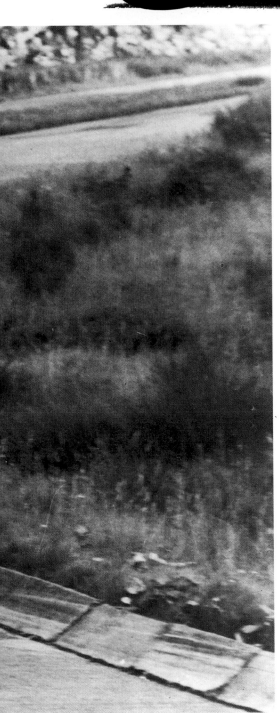

Spring 1952: in the Grand Jubilee Prize for sports cars, Hermann Lang in the Mercedes 300SL prototype has an easy win. This was the first event entered after the war by the Mercedes racing department with the corpulent Alfred Neubauer as their "impresario." The Mathé light alloy Porsche (top left) may well have been the fastest 1.5 liter sports car in 1954. Top right: The Borgward RS of 1954, a very rare beast which often outperformed the Porsches and Ferraris

changes were to be expected in each race, and generally the tire depot was a long way from the track. So the driver and mechanic simply had to spit on their blood–stained hands and get down to work. No one could match the strongest man in the Mercedes team, Otto Merz, who could knock four-inch nails into a plank with the flat of his hand and lift the 33 cwt (1676 kg) of the Mercedes SSK when a wheel was to be changed, so that the mechanics simply had to shove a jack under the axle. Otto's strength reduced the usual time for a tire change from 3 minutes to 90 seconds. The team manager Alfred Neubauer recalls in his memoirs that Merz once shook the delicate Baroness Wentzel–Mossau's hand with such force that her valuable but rather bent wedding ring could only be removed with a pair of pliers.

For all their strength, the German team suffered a wipeout in the race. Tommy Milton won in his Miller HCS at an average speed of 90.95 mph (146.34 kph), while the best Mercedes works driver was Max Sailer back in 8th place. Prince de Cystria in the fastest Bugatti was a lap further back in 9th place. The defeated Mercedes team returned to Germany somewhat disillusioned on the Hapag liner, without their racing cars. The transport costs for the three cars would have exceeded the budget for the race. The reason for the failure of these first supercharged racers was probably that they were very difficult to drive: the 40 percent boost in power came in with a bang. As the new chief designer, Ferdinand Porsche took the further development of the model in hand, and in their next important race the supercharged cars were successful.

One of the most important races of 1924 was the Targa Florio in Sicily. Everyone who was anyone came. As usual the Mercedes racing team drove

The Felber Ferrari FF: a cross between a Grand Prix car and a street legal supersports car

D·RE 931

STIRLING MOSS, THE RACING GENIUS OF HIS TIME

down to Sicily from Stuttgart under their own steam to cut down on traveling expenses. After four days they at last reached Rome. And it took these experienced racing drivers 11 hours to cover the last 150 miles (240 km) to Naples, where the boat for Sicily was waiting for them. One can imagine the road conditions and the stifling heat in Sicily. Neubauer recalls: "The sun beats down mercilessly, the wind cuts into one's face without any cooling effect. Dust gets into one's mouth and nose, into every pore, and covers one's face with a black mask. After two laps the skin on my fingers is already torn to shreds and my hands are covered in blood, pounded by the constant kicking of the steering wheel. Once again comes the bitter realization that the racing driver at the wheel is the loneliest person in the world."

The Targa Florio of 1924 played a decisive role in the history of motor sport for two reasons. The then Mercedes works driver Alfred Neubauer invented the role of team manager, and the supercharged engine came of age. Neubauer's talent for organization developed alongside his legendary physical bulk. In future many races were to be won by him in the pits. His mechanics loved him, but they also feared him for his furious outbursts. He once said to one of his best mechanics at the German Grand Prix on the Nürburgring "You're so stupid you couldn't even make Spätzle", which is the worst possible insult for anyone from Stuttgart.

The victory in the Targa Florio was the real breakthrough for the supercharged engine. Up to the Second World War supercharged cars were to be victorious in every important race. With the building of permanent high-speed circuits such as the Avus in Berlin or the banked course at

Stirling Moss in his best period was the fastest of the fast drivers. From 1951 to 1961 he took pole position 16 times, put up the fastest lap 20 times and won 16 Grands Prix, for the most part in cars with an inferior performance. From 1955 to 1958 he had the frustration of always being the runner–up in the World Championship, but everyone knew that the older drivers were often given preference by the team managers. His dream of becoming a Ferrari works driver was never fulfilled. Moss gave up racing in 1962 after a serious accident in his Lotus–Climax

On high–speed circuits such as Rheims and Monza the streamlined Mercedes W196 was way ahead of the competition. The disadvantages of the wide bodywork became only too obvious on narrow twisting courses (see painting below). Consequently Fangio could do no better than 4th place in the British Grand Prix behind the Ferraris and Maseratis

MERCEDES-BENZ

erringt in hartem Kampf gegen internationale Konkurrenz einen
überlegenen Doppelsieg im

GROSSEN PREIS VON FRANKREICH 1954

1. Juan Manuel Fangio
2. Karl Kling

GRAND PRIX D'EUROPE AUTOMOBILE

MONACO
22 MAI 1955
CHAMPIONNAT DU MONDE DES CONDUCTEURS
XIIIe GRAND PRIX AUTOMOBILE DE MONACO
Prix : 100 Frs

PROGRAMME OFFICIEL

41E GRAND PRIX
DE L'A.C.F.
REIMS
4 JUILLET 1954

PROGRAMME OFFICIEL   PRIX : 100 FR.

In 1979 Jody Scheckter left the competition trailing in the wake of his Ferrari 312 T4, and won for Ferrari what has so far been their last world championship, with team mate Gilles Villeneuve in second place who had three wins to his credit. The 12 cylinder Ferrari 312 T4 is a typical ground effect car. The side skirts almost touch the track and provide increased downward pressure and thus higher cornering speeds. Skirts are now prohibited as a result of numerous accidents. When passing over a bad bump in the road surface the pressure is suddenly reduced and the car literally takes off

In 1955 Mercedes won both the Constructors' and (with Fangio) the Drivers' World Championships. However in Monaco (right) all three Mercedes retired, although they were initially leading the race. Maurice Trintignant won for Ferrari, with Castelotti second in the Lancia with the side tanks

RETURN OF MERCEDES IN 1954:
1–2 FOR FANGIO IN NO. 18
AND KLING IN NO. 20

The young Stirling Moss (top) was not permitted to challenge seriously the world champion Fangio (lower picture), who was considerably his senior. The Mercedes team manager Alfred Neubauer (in the hat) was constantly checking that his decisions were being carried out. The better aerodynamic shape of the Mercedes Grand Prix cars as compared to their rivals is very obvious in this shot of the 1954 French GP (above)

Monza near Milan, race driving became a real profession. The Nürburgring acquired the reputation of being a killer circuit for both men and machines. In almost every race at least one driver died as a result of technical defects or driver error. Gone were the days of drivers with prodigious strength like Otto Merz. What were wanted now were polished and stylish practitioners of the art of driving. Motor racing became a social event in the 1930s which VIPs from industry, the arts, and politics liked to attend. From 1933 onward in Germany the Nazi bosses intervened on a massive scale on the racing scene. But more of that later.

Tire development could not keep up with the ever increasing speeds of the Grand Prix racers. At the high–speed Avus race on August 2, 1931, the Continental tires were only lasting for four laps in practice. However the Mercedes works drivers (and nobody else) had six new tires with a harder compound, and Rudolf Caracciola used these to win. Neubauer was publicly accused of cheating and favoritism and summoned to the Transport Ministry. Politics versus motor sport. Luckily for Neubauer, the chief designer Dr Nibel stood by his team manager and saved him from any unpleasant consequences.

In 1937 Hermann Lang achieved a record practice lap at Avus of 177.3 mph (283.7 kph) and won at an average speed of 163.6 mph (261.7 kph). A fantastic performance. The Grand Prix cars of those days were hardly any slower than today's racers. The C type 16 cylinder Auto Union with the new centrally mounted engine giving 520 bhp was clocked in 1936 at the Tripoli Grand Prix at a top speed of 196 mph (314 kph). In 1937 Mercedes quoted 600 bhp for their new 8 cylinder W125. This front–engined racer with

Revolutionary: the General Motors XP21 Firebird, America's first gas turbine racing car (right). Flop: 12 cylinder 6 liter Panhard giving 200 bhp (far right)

SHOCK TO THE SYSTEM
– A GREEN DAVID SLAYS
A RED GOLIATH

Although Fangio was still able to win his fifth championship title in 1957 in the front–engined Maserati 250F, the British "garage proprietors" astonished their rivals with some sensational lap times. The dainty mid–engined racing Cooper–Climax (top left) only had 198 bhp available, but on the other hand it only weighed 8 cwt 26 lbs (417 kg). It ran its first race at Monaco in 1957. In 1959 Jack Brabham won the World Championship in it in convincing fashion. The first Lotus Formula 1 racing car (left), with a four cylinder 2207 cc front–mounted Climax engine, dates from 1958

a top speed of 211 mph won seven of the 13 races for which it was entered. Alfa Romeo, Bugatti, ERA, MG and Maserati could only win in their national races, which did not count for the European Championship with its 750 kg formula. For reasons of cost, most of these respected racing car firms competed with smaller engined cars of at most 3 to 4 liters, whereas the Auto Union C type had 6010 cc and the Mercedes W125 5660 cc under the silver hood.

Hitler and his propaganda minister Goebbels regarded the Grand Prix races as an excellent vehicle for their expansionist aims and enlisted the aid of an assiduously subservient automobile industry. Auto Union and Mercedes each received advances of about 470,000 marks for designing and building new racing cars (about five million marks or three million dollars in today's money). The Mercedes works drivers could be well satisfied with a guaranteed salary of 120,000 marks and a bonus of 20,000 marks for first place, 15,000 marks for second, and 10,000 marks for third. Expenses for racing and practice were paid at a rate of 40 marks, in addition to which a car was supplied for private use free of charge. But neither the triple European champion Rudolf Caracciola nor Manfred von Brauchitsch from Mercedes, nor the brilliant Bernd Rosemeyer from Auto Union was a really big earner at the end of the 1930s. That was the distinction reserved for the great hillclimb champion Hans Stuck. With a guaranteed sum of 150,000 marks he exceeded all previous salary demands as the last top German driver to join Auto Union. But the Second World War put an end to all racing in Europe, and this glorious era of motor sport came to an abrupt close.

■

THE GRAND PRIX CIRCUS TAKES OFF

The successful slender British mid–engined racing cars increase the chances but also the risks for the driver

Ken Tyrrell, owner of a small racing team, hit the jackpot when he picked the Scot Jackie Stewart, who was exceptionally fast both in the dry and in the wet, as here at Barcelona in 1971. Three world championship titles, 5,640 miles (9,077 km) at the front of the race, 1893 laps in the lead. He still has star status

Graham Hill drove his first race in 1958 in the fragile Lotus 11 (top left). He was world champion in 1962 and 1968 with BRM and Lotus. The likable old campaigner died in 1975 when flying his own plane. With 16 bad crashes between 1974 and 1979, James Hunt (center left) had a reputation for taking risks. Hunt was world champion in 1976 driving for McLaren–Ford

Pedro Rodriguez (above) and his brother Ricardo were extremely fast but very eccentric Latin exotics. Ricardo died in 1962 driving for the Ferrari works team. Pedro met his death in 1971 in the Noris–Rennen at Nuremberg in a prototype Ferrari. The rescue services were unable to save him from his burning car

Mark Donohue won the Indianapolis 500 Mile Race in 1972 and was the big white hope of the Penske team. In 1975 he had a fatal accident at Zeltweg due to tire failure

Ronnie Peterson died in 1978 in a pile-up at Monza; the medical services were inadequate

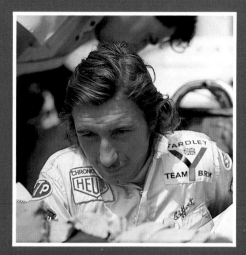

The Swiss Jo Siffert won the hearts of the spectators with his tremendous enthusiasm. In 1971 he had a fatal accident at Brands Hatch due to material failure

For 20 years Colin Chapman and his Lotus racers were a byword for brilliant ideas. But his rivals did not take it lying down, and from 1979 to 1984 the Lotuses were no longer dominant. The black John Player Lotus 95T was a further attempt to regain supremacy which enjoyed some success, but never won the Constructors' Championship

The Swedish Grand Prix
of 1978 is an example of
how ingenious designers
are repeatedly stymied
by the governing body of
motor sport, the CSI. Niki
Lauda turned up in
Anderstorp with a
"vacuum cleaner" on his
Brabham–Alfa BT46. The
fan is driven from the
gearbox mainshaft,
producing a vacuum
beneath the sealed
underbody which sucks
the car down onto the
track. The result was
that Lauda won, but the
device was immediately
banned

Only two examples of the four–wheel drive Lotus Ford 63 were raced in 1969. Graham Hill and Jochen Rindt complained about the difficult handling

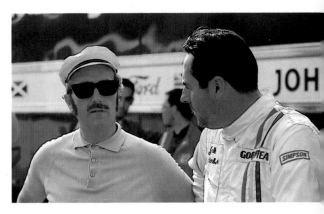

Colin Chapman (left), the owner of Lotus, and his rival Jack Brabham. The two got on very well with one another, although they both made their living from motor sport

The twin shaft Pratt & Whitney gas turbine walked away with the Indianapolis 500 Mile Race, but it could not make good use of its superior output of 475 bhp at 45,000 rpm on the twisty Grand Prix circuits. The turbine is also used in military helicopters. Kerosene consumption about 3 mpg (1 km per liter), double the fuel consumption of a piston engine

The gas turbine Lotus 56B (right) was the sensation of 1971. Extremely high fuel consumption, four–wheel drive and overheating brakes led to its failure

HIGH TECH IN 1971 – FOUR–WHEEL DRIVE AND GAS TURBINE POWER

Perhaps, dear reader, you have at some time had the following dream: it's the night before the British Grand Prix and along with a few hundred other fans you are camping in a small tent. You watch in your dream a breathtaking dingdong between world champion Ayrton Senna and Nigel Mansell, his perpetual rival. Alain Prost hovers like a vulture waiting to pounce a car's length behind. What happens next is almost unbelievable. A slim blue Lotus fights its way through the field from the back of the pack. The driver of the privately entered car has a white cross on his red helmet and overtakes the established stars in spectacular fashion. This unknown then wins the British Grand Prix by half a car's length. What you have dreamed actually happened in the sixties. In 1968 to be precise, the Swiss Jo Siffert, one of the "poorest" private entrants, won the British Grand Prix at Brands Hatch. Driving the Rob Walker Team's privately entered Lotus Ford, which was hardly competitive in terms of power, he beat the Ferrari works drivers Chris Amon and Jacky Ickx, and left Dennis Hulme (McLaren), John Surtees (Honda) and Jackie Stewart (Matra–Ford) trailing. This was no easy victory, but a hard fight all the way. The other finishers from second down to sixth place were all, or were to become, Formula 1 world champions – with the exception of Chris Amon, who even so had five pole positions to his credit.

It was a crazy time. The big earners sat in their Ferraris and looked askance at the British teams run by John Cooper and Colin Chapman with their tubby Cooper BRMs and the filigree Lotus Climaxes. A few private teams took their chances with both hands. The low–cost 1.5 liter Formula 1 enabled the small teams to compete in ten

The 70s brought to Formula 1 for the first time sponsorship money, which enabled even small racing car manufacturers to produce and race technically advanced racers, such as this 12 cylinder Tecno PA123 made by the Peterzani brothers. Nanni Galli and Derek Bell never managed to achieve higher than middle placings

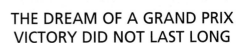

Most teams in 1972 put their faith in the V8 Ford DFV. Emerson Fittipaldi became world champion driving the Lotus 72D which was fitted with

it. Ferrari, Matra, BRM and Tecno were more attracted to 12 cylinder engines. Tecno's low "semi–flat" 12 had six journals for 12 connecting rods. Clay Regazzoni won many races with the Tecno F2 (right) in 1970

THE DREAM OF A GRAND PRIX VICTORY DID NOT LAST LONG

Grand Prix races and numerous others which did not count for the World Championship. Nearly all the famous British racing outfits have their origins in this 1.5 liter formula.

The Lotus, Cooper, Brabham and BRM, which only weighed about 1,000 pounds or less than 9 cwt (450 kg), were the typical underdogs as compared with the established makes such as Ferrari and Porsche. The superior handling of these smart "babies" made the considerably more powerful Ferraris appear somewhat elderly on narrow street courses such as Monaco. But Enzo Ferrari still spoke dismissively of the British "garage proprietors" who wanted to submit entries. Pride comes before a fall.

In 1961 the world championship was again won in a Ferrari, by Phil Hill, with Graf Berghe von Trips in second place, who was fatally injured at Monza. But only a year later Graham Hill in his BRM became the first driver of one of these garage proprietors' products to be world champion. BRM had the magnificent total of 42 world championship points. Ferrari's 18 points were regarded as a national disaster in Italy. The British teams really made a killing: Lotus had 36 points, Cooper 29, while Lola, Porsche and Ferrari were level on 18. With only six points Jack Brabham was propping up the bottom of the table with his own design.

The British mechanics and drivers slept in their vans or tents behind the pits, while the Italian Grand Prix elite had rooms in the best hotels. It was only too evident that there was a two–class society. Because the British teams were always desperately short of money, they sold all their worn out cars to private racing teams. Even the latest models suffered for years from material failures such as would be unthinkable in Formula 1 today. With the introduction of the 3 liter

JUST OVER 150 YARDS TO THE FIRST CORNER. SPEED 150 MPH (240 KPH) – PULSE RATE 200

Grand Prix racing has never stopped developing. In 1969 only 16 cars competed for the world championship, and a year later 30 drivers had their sights on the victor's laurels. The then new firm March provided a dozen drivers with suitable machinery. In the French Grand Prix Mario Andretti in the STP March 701 survived this accident in spite of rolling over three times, because there was no wall in the way

formula in 1966 the number of accidents escalated, caused by the frequent material failures. In 1968 the ruling body for motor sport permitted advertising on the cars and drivers' clothing. Technically less fastidious racing car manufacturers were now tempted to make risky reductions in weight at the expense of safety. The number of accidents in 1970 shows only the tip of the iceberg. Piers Courage burnt to death at Zandvoort as a result of a suspension breakage; Jochen Rindt died at Monza because of a broken brake shaft; and Bruce McLaren met his death in his CanAm racer due to a wheel bearing failure.

Because the small amounts of starting and prize money paid barely covered the teams' living costs, all the Grand Prix drivers also competed in the less popular races. In those days, the Formula 1 privateer Jo Siffert had 40 races per year on his busy schedule. He drove for BMW in the European Formula 2 Championship, won almost every race in the long–distance world championship for John Wyer's Porsche team, and shocked the McLarens which were used to having things all their own way with his privately entered Porsche 917 CanAm car.

Then in 1971 in the last Formula 1 race of the year at Brands Hatch on October 24th, 1971, Siffert was fighting for the lead with Ronnie Peterson, Fittipaldi, Stewart and Gethin. At Hawthorn Bend Jo's car suddenly shot off at a sharp angle into the earth bank. The car rolled over and burst into flames – there was no possibility of a rescue. Jackie Stewart saw the accident. His comment says it all: "There can be no question of Siffert having made a mistake. At the point where the accident happened he did not even have to brake." ∎

THE TURBO ERA – UNDERPOWERED WITH 1,000 BHP

Renault attempted the impossible and won. The 1.5 liter turbocharged engine was soon beating normally aspirated engines of twice the size

The Renault Gordini V6 engine of 1977 weighing 400 pounds (180 kg) at the time of its first outing in England. Its 520 bhp as compared to the 485 bhp of the Ford Cosworth was impressive, but the conventional 8 and 12 cylinder cars were more pleasant to drive, as there was no "turbo lag" to get in the way. In the next five years the output of the turbocharged engines increased to way over 1,000 bhp

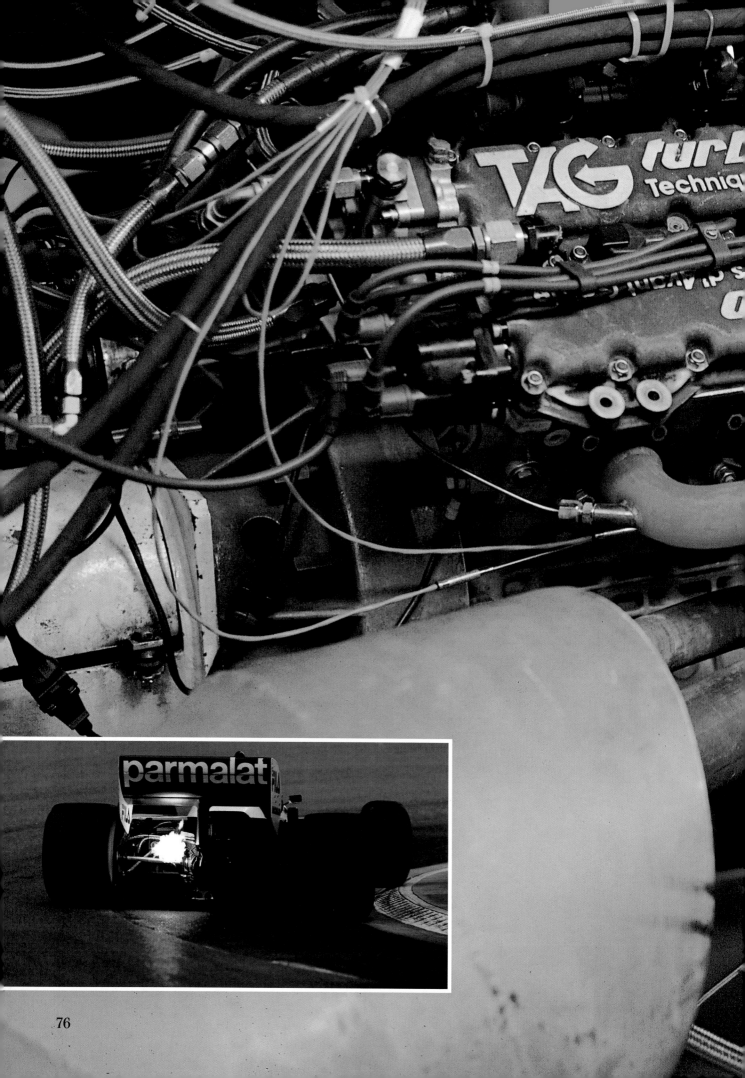

The great successes of the German turbo experts are already past history. In 1983 Nelson Piquet won the world championship with the Brabham BT52B (below). Paul Rosche's 4 cylinder BMW M12/13 turbo reached nearly 1200 bhp with the prescribed capacity of 1,500 cc. Porsche's reputation as the best builder of racing engines was confirmed in 1984 with Hans Mezger's 6 cylinder TAG turbo fitted to the McLaren. For three years Lauda and Prost gave the opposition a hard time

The 1.5 liter Ferrari 126C engine of 1984 is a V6 with two KKK turbochargers. To improve cooling three to six percent water was injected into the petrol/air mixture. The result was lower consumption and maximum turbo boost with acceptable temperature levels

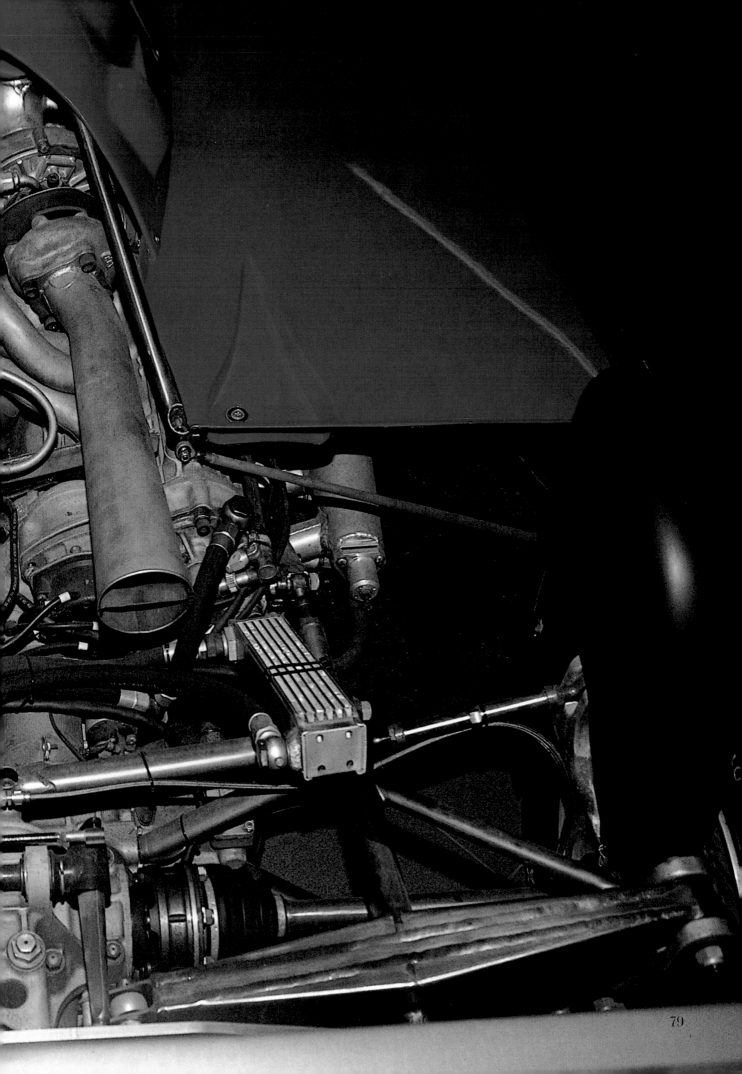

The German Zakspeed team took on the world's elite with much courage but little financial backing. They were denied any higher placings by minor problems in the engine management system. The withdrawal of their sponsor meant the end of the road for the German Formula 1 protagonists

FORMULA 1 ZAKSPEED: A SMALL TEAM WITH BIG ASPIRATIONS

The European racing world looked enviously in the direction of America in the mid–sixties. There the Indianapolis winner could usually earn over 180,000 dollars, while in Europe 24,000 dollars (£16,000) was the most one could earn in prize money for a Grand Prix victory. The new 3 liter formula promised to be more attractive, which took over in 1966 and remained in force until 1989. No other racing formula developed such a self–perpetuating dynamic. In order to give the designers even more scope, the French team bosses had supercharged 1.5 liter engines included in the regulations. This was to give the 4 cylinder engines of the previous 1,500 cc formula a chance of survival. Turbocharging as a technique was only known at that time in shipbuilding, but supercharging had been used successfully since the twenties.

Today we can see that it was due to this rider to the regulations that Formula 1 saw an explosive increase in output to figures over 1,200 bhp from 1.5 liters. A VW Golf engine with this capacity develops only 65 bhp. But neither Ford nor Ferrari, nor Porsche, nor Alfa Romeo saw supercharging as an alternative with any chance against the ideally compact and reliable Ford Cosworth V8 or the beautiful Ferrari flat 12. Only two radical outsiders put their faith in the smaller 1.5 liter engine with turbocharging: Renault and Honda. Their design concept was treated with scorn and derision for years by the experts, but in the end they got their nose in front – after all one only sees the fruits of persistent development work in motor racing after a matter of years – and today Honda and Renault enjoy an unchallenged position in this field. It took quite some courage to take on the established 3 liter opposition. The statistics show

The 1985 season began with a flourish for the German fans. The West Zakspeed 841 had its second race at Monaco (left) proved itself to be competitive with the compact 850 bhp 4 cylinder turbocharged engine, which they had developed themselves. On its debut it achieved 10th place with "Doc" Palmer at the wheel

Not only his boss Ken
Tyrrell saw in Stefan
Bellof (right) a future
world champion. In his
20 Grand Prix races the
driver from Giessen took
many a star down a peg
or two. Stefan died at the
age of 27 in the Spa
1000 Kilometers as a
result of driver error in
the Bruns–Porsche 956

AUTUMN 1985: FATE STRIKES THOSE WHO LEAST DESERVE IT

the overwhelming superiority of the 3 liter
engines at the time.

The series of victories scored by the 3 liter Ford
Cosworth engine began in 1968 with Graham Hill
in his Lotus Ford and only came to an end in
1982 with Keke Rosberg in the Williams–Ford.
The three titles won by Ferrari in this period
(1975, 1977, 1979) were down to Niki Lauda
(two wins) and Jody Scheckter with the normally
aspirated 3,000 cc engine. This means that the 3
liter Ford Cosworth was the most successful
Grand Prix engine of all time. Even so its days
were numbered as the new 12 cylinder Ford
3500 was race–ready.

If one traces the development of the 1.5 liter
turbocharged engine back to its early days, one
comes upon a secret testing session on the Paul
Ricard Circuit in the spring of 1975. The Renault
works driver Patrick Depailler was putting in
some remarkably fast laps in a blue Formula 2
Martini–Renault. It was driven by a turbocharged
V6 engine at the rear. The fastest lap would have
been good enough for sixth place on the grid in
the French Grand Prix. Renault gave the green
light for further development.

For the British Grand Prix of 1977 Renault laid
their cards on the table; they entered
Jean–Pierre Jabouille in a new car with a much
improved engine. Renault gave its power output
as 520 to 530 bhp as compared to the 480 or so
of the Ford engines. They set the stakes high and
then lost. My colleague Ulrich Schwab was
present at this first appearance and soberly
recorded in his Grand Prix yearbook what others
had described as a disaster: "The problems with
the engine were many and varied. They began
with a series of breakages of the forged
short–skirt pistons, continued with valve and
bearing trouble, and ended with the behavior

Manfred Winkelhock (top
left) died in the Group C
Kremer–Porsche 962 in
circumstances which
have so far never been
satisfactorily explained.
In the ATS–BMW (left)
the 32-year-old only gave
sporadic evidence of his
undoubted talent in his
47 Formula 1 races.
Problems within the team
and financial difficulties
inhibited the likable
fellow from Waiblingen
near Stuttgart in his
much too brief career

Bernie Ecclestone   Niki Lauda   Frank Williams

THREE GREAT MEN ARE MORE EFFECTIVE THAN 99 OFFICIALS

Probably the strongest personality among the drivers of the last 15 years has been the Austrian Niki Lauda (top center). In addition to his undoubted qualities as a driver, one should single out the masterly way in which the three times world champion handles the media. His pronouncements have been respected. His own terrible experiences in the burning Ferrari on the Nürburgring made him into a passionate crusader for improved safety. Andrea de Cesaris probably owes his survival in this high–speed crash in the warm–up for the 1983 San Marino Grand Prix to the new safety regulations

typical of engines with this type of boost, the so–called turbocharger effect: too little power when you want it, and too much when you don't. While the Renault served mainly as a testbed for its constructors and Michelin, its rivals had to earn their living."

Finally the problems were solved. From 1977 to 1982 the Renault turbo had 128 starts, with 11 victories, 13 lap records and 27 pole positions. These may sound good, but a win in the world championship was denied to Renault for other reasons. Even so, from 1984 all the big teams ran with turbos on the Renault principle.

In 1984 the Formula 1 circus experienced the shock of the irresistible rise of the Brazilian Ayrton Senna da Silva in the British Toleman team. With a new carbon fiber chassis and the Hart turbocharged engine, Senna was able to command respect.

In the 1984 Monaco Grand Prix the Brazilian challenged the world's elite in the wet. Niki Lauda and Alain Prost headed the field with their McLaren Porsche MP4/2s. Starting from 13th place on the grid, Senna overtook one driver after another. On lap 19 Senna was pursuing the several times world champion Niki Lauda when Lauda span in front of the Hotel de Paris and retired. Now Senna attacked Alain Prost, clinging to the Frenchman's tail. Then, incredibly, race director Jacky Ickx stopped the race in response to Alain Prost's desperate signals, although the conditions had not deteriorated any further. Senna was therefore second, one second behind. Ickx was accused of cheating by the press and some of the team bosses. Ayrton Senna had given the established stars something to think about. "I wanted to spare the car and therefore drove with more restraint than I could have done." The barb went home. ∎

FORMULA 1 ON THE ROAD TO NOWHERE

The two–class society: Nigel Mansell collects the money while Paul Belmondo pays for the drive

From 1984 to 1991 every Drivers' World Championship was won in a McLaren, except in 1987. The McLaren MP4/2 as driven by Niki Lauda has been continuously developed

The small teams make for added interest. McKechnie Racing only managed places in the middle of the field, which was not good enough to survive in this, the most costly form of racing

There goes another 200,000 dollars (£132,000) worth of Ferrari engine. For years the whole of Italy has been waiting for one of the red 12 cylinder racers to win a race. Management mistakes and disagreements in the team have allowed McLaren and Williams to gain a big lead. The Benetton team have shown with the less powerful Ford V8 engine that horsepower isn't everything

World champion Alain
Prost left Ferrari in 1991
after a row. Niki Lauda
was brought in to
coordinate the interests
of the team and those of
the drivers

The 1991 double-
bottomed Ferrari
designed by Harvey
Postlethwaite in the
South African Grand
Prix. Ivan Capelli's first
drive ended with engine
failure after a good start

The new pits complex at Kyalami in South Africa. The McLaren–Hondas of Senna and Berger are ready to go, while most of the other teams are wasting valuable minutes of practice time. Vital preparations are made in practice for victory in the race. In the background the blue Jordan–Yamaha of Gugelmin is coming down the pit lane; it has a 12 cylinder engine with 5 valves per cylinder

YELLOW PAGES

Formula 1 is now safer
than any other race
category. Over a period
of eight years and 154
Grand Prix races there
has not been a single
fatal accident. All new
race circuits are provided
with wide run–off areas.
Previously there were
crash barriers at such
danger spots. Reporter
from Japan (left)
complete with sun
helmet, Nikon and mobile
telephone

MEDIA HEADQUARTERS: FORMULA 1 PUBLICITY FOR FREE

The two most important men in the Grand Prix business are Bernie Ecclestone (top left), the head of FOCA (Formula One Constructors' Association), and Ron Dennis, McLaren team manager. Riccardo Patrese (center), the Williams and Benetton driver with well over 200 Grand Prix races to his credit. Some recent Formula 1 cars on the left; from top to bottom, the Tyrrell–Ilmor 2175A V10 driven by Zanardi; the Ligier–Renault with Boutsen at the wheel; the Scuderia Italia Dallara BMS with Ferrari V12 engine; and the Martini–Footwork–Mugen –Honda B10 driven by Alboreto. The Gilles Villeneuve memorial stone in Imola. Secret: McLaren's tire–heating apparatus

The Formula 1 world championship is going flat out into bankruptcy. This prediction of imminent disaster comes up every five years or so in the mass circulation magazines. At the moment the smaller teams are in fact haunted by the specter of insolvency, because the coffers are empty and sponsors with checkbooks at the ready are becoming increasingly rare. Only five out of 17 teams had the same main sponsors in 1992 as in 1991. In spite of this gloomy outlook, Formula 1 is still the sporting fixture with the highest TV ratings after the Olympic Games according to figures published by the Formula 1 Constructors' Association.

There are reasons for this. Today's sport for the masses thrives on the scandals concerning those involved. Race victories are soon forgotten but disreputable affairs stay in the memory. Porsche's embarrassing Formula 1 episode with their partner Footwork in the 1991 season caused more of a stir than their three world championship wins in association with McLaren in the turbo era. Another example was the question of whether Mercedes would return to Formula 1. This issue brought the Stuttgart concern 132 times more attention in the media than the hard fought sports car races in which they competed, according to a marketing agency. The dramatic row at Ferrari with their one–time ideal partner, multiple world champion Alain Prost, also did the Fiat concern more good than harm, because it fitted in with Ferrari's aggressive image. Which all goes to show that being in the limelight is more important than sporting achievement.

Stirling Moss put his finger on it: "Ten years ago motor racing was a sport, today motor racing is a business." At present only four teams have the resources to fight out the merciless "arms race".

99

No team can have been so deserving of success as the British team run by Frank Williams. Back in the seventies, even 10th place was an achievement. By 1992 the Williams–Renault V10 driven by Nigel Mansell (above) and Riccardo Patrese were the most innovative racing cars around, with semi automatic transmission, active suspension, an antislip acceleration system (which prevents the driven wheels from spinning at the start), and the most effective aerodynamics in Formula 1

WILLIAMS–RENAULT, THE YARDSTICK FOR THE COMPETITION

They are the big names in the business: McLaren with their partner Honda, Williams with the state–owned Renault as engine supplier, Ferrari as part of the big Fiat combine, and (suffering cutbacks) Benetton supported by the Ford Motor Company. The other twelve teams inevitably remain no more than also-rans. The worldwide recession in the automobile industry will however soon affect the financially strong teams as well. The golden years of the eighties are already past history.

The other factor is the lack of any real personalities among the drivers. At present only four stars are really well known: ex–world champion Ayrton Senna, his former rival Nigel Mansell, world champion Alain Prost, and (particularly in Germany) the 24-year-old German hope Michael Schumacher, who rocketed to fame in 1991 and was the undisputed favorite of the German public in 1992–3.

Should dyed in the wool enthusiasts get excited as they try to decipher the names of Japanese racing drivers such as Ukyo Katayama or Aguri Suzuki, thinking here might be a sensational driving talent? No way. A good 50 percent of the current Formula 1 drivers are behind the wheel not because of their driving ability but because millions have been paid out to put them there. When several times world champions such as Alain Prost and Nelson Piquet are without a drive for the 1992 season and the film star's son Paul Belmondo gets a starting permit, then there is something wrong with Bernie Ecclestone's Grand Prix business empire.

The trouble lies in the rocketing costs, which are forcing all the smaller racing teams to their knees. The ban on cigarette advertising in 1993 meant that the top teams had to look elsewhere

THE BACKMARKERS WHO WANT TO GET IN FRONT

Christian Fittipaldi in the Minardi–Lamborghini V12 (top left) – the third member of the Fittipaldi family in a Formula 1 cockpit. Jordan–Yamaha V12 (center): Mauricio Gugelmin hopes to bring new fame to the marine engine manufacturer. Venturi Larrousse–Lamborghini V12 driven by Bertrand Gachot (top), basis of a small but ambitious team. Simply competing is what counts: the Fondmetal–Ford V8 with Gabriele Tarquini (large picture). Millions spent for the last place on the grid

for sponsorship. Some of the proposed EC legislation also makes one fear the worst for Formula 1. In the USA, Canada and Mexico similar punitive measures are being considered, including a ban on advertising alcohol. At Marlboro, a Philip Morris subsidiary and the biggest sponsor of motor sport, serious consideration is being given to abandoning all involvement in motor sport. Both in Formula 1 with McLaren–Honda and in Indy racing with the Roger Penske team, Marlboro have so far been responsible for an inexhaustible supply of money. All Grand Prix races in the last ten years received massive support from Marlboro. Camel have already reduced their involvement in motor sport considerably, and Gitanes are also thinking of giving up motor sport advertising. Does this mean curtains for the Grand Prix circus? It is a well known phenomenon that those whose death is foretold live longer. This category of racing will continue to exert its fascination for all enthusiasts; after all the world's best drivers are only found in Formula 1. Radical changes in the regulations are inevitable, since the cost–benefit ratio even makes the publicity men go red with embarrassment. With a new set of regulations aimed at reducing costs it will even be possible for the less affluent teams to engage drivers solely for their driving ability.
If Renault and Ferrari currently calculate the cost of an engine to be 200,000 dollars (£132,000), this must give even notorious optimists food for thought. Ferrari currently has a stock of 120 racing engines! The commitment of Honda and Renault is equal in extent. Such gigantic costs are not affordable in the long term.
 In future 90,000 dollars (£60,000) is to be the limit for a racing engine producing 700 bhp. Then it will no longer cost 300 million dollars (£200

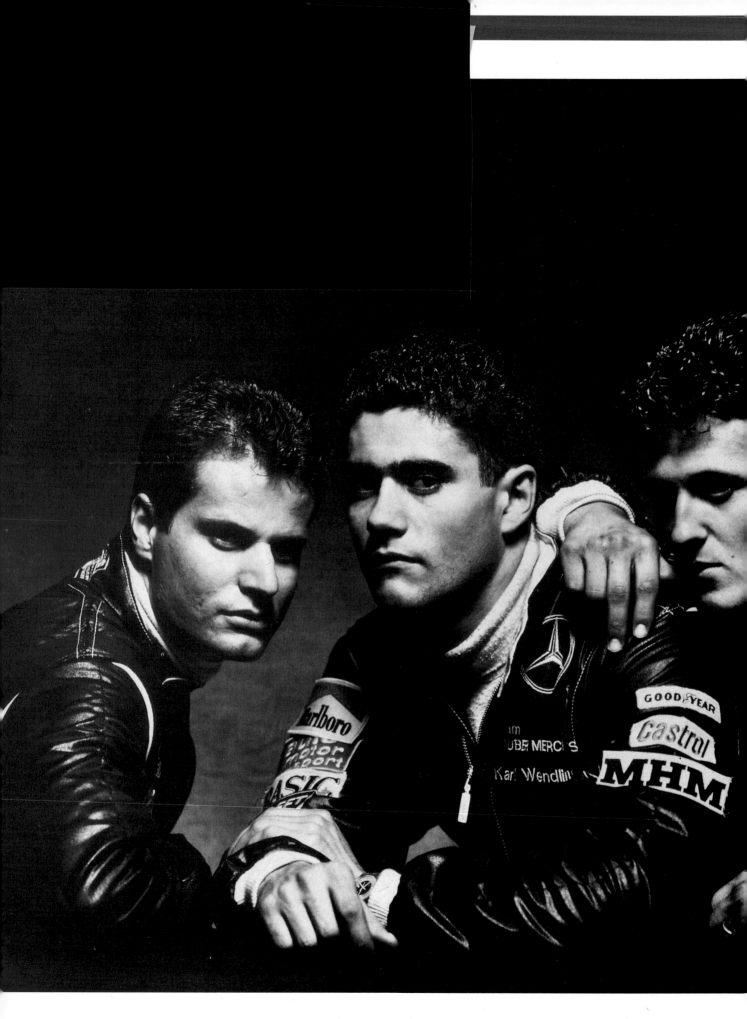

SHOOTING STARS
"MIKE" SCHUMACHER AND KARL WENDLINGER

million) to run a team for a season, as is the ca
with McLaren, but something in the region of
to 30 million dollars (£8 to £20 million). If the
are no changes in the regulations, Honda,
Renault and Ford will withdraw from Formula
in the next three years, as no firm can afford
cream off its best engineers for racing engine
development over a long period. And then s
scale manufacturers such as Mario Illien wil
have their chance.

Finally the pressure of public opinion on Fo
1 racing will increase rather than decrease
Anomalies such as the removal of the regu
on quantity and type of fuel are to blame f
Racing mechanics already have to wear
protective face masks and fireproof overa
when filling the tanks, because the fuels
concocted in the secret laboratories are
extremely poisonous and also highly exp
The nonpoisonous methanol would be th
sensible alternative to the present witch
In the Indianapolis 500 Mile Race metha
been used as fuel for years, since the g
fumes are a danger to the spectators.
probably only a question of time before
Greenpeace or one of the other conservationist
organizations tries to stop a Grand Prix race.
The receipts from spectators are still an
important item in Bernie Ecclestone's budget.
And yet there are increasing signs that it is only
the sponsors with their millions who call the tune
in the Grand Prix circus.

It must have been clear to everyone involved
when Mercedes decided against entering the lists
of Formula 1, if not before, that Formula 1 has to
be redefined, otherwise the world's most
successful series of races will soon be faced with
the prospect of a final closedown.   ∎

Mercedes racing manager Jochen Neerpasch catapulted his two fastest youngsters Michael Schumacher (right) and Karl Wendlinger (center) from sports car racing straight into Formula 1. Fritz Kreutzpointner (left) is still being blooded in touring car racing. Schumacher drove the yellow Benetton–Ford in his first full Grand Prix season in 1992, while Wendlinger had the March–Ilmor

EASTERN EUROPE: A NEW DAWN

Reunification is also taking place on the race circuits.
Hot cars instead of the cold war

MOTOR RACING UNDER STATE CONTROL

For decades the car and motorcycle races in Eastern Europe were regarded as second–rate motor sport. In fact the spectators there often get more action for their entrance money than we do in the west. The photographs were taken at the first event after the opening of the German frontier, the race meeting on the Schleiz Triangle. The attractively designed Formula E racing cars correspond more or less to West European Formula 3 cars, having a capacity of 1600 cc

The fastest Formula E racing cars, such as this white Melkus from the former GDR, are just as attractive as their western counterparts. In the far background is a Russian Volga. The most successful Formula E drivers for many years used American Goodyear or Japanese Bridgestone racing tires with the approval of the party bosses, and rubbed off the name of the capitalist manufacturer. Today an entirely pragmatic view is taken of the tire question. Hard currency is used to buy the best

FASCINATING PICTURES FROM ANOTHER WORLD

Sixty–four thousand dollar question: which is the oldest race circuit in Germany? The Avus perhaps, or the Nürburgring, or even Hockenheim? All wrong. The races at the Schleiz Triangle in eastern Thuringia have been going on for 70 years. The "first fuel test drive" for motorcycles took place on June 10, 1923. The aim was to cover the greatest possible distance on five liters of gasoline. The first German "road champion" was Toni Bauhofer from Munich on his 5 cylinder Megola.

Apart from the war years when there was no racing, there have been 58 international events here and countless national races. The Schleiz circuit is a cross between the old Nürburgring and the former high–speed circuit at Spa in Belgium. Since the addition of a new chicane the Schleiz Triangle is now 4.23 miles (6.805 km) long. The lap record was held until 1990 by the Czech Miran Velkoborsky in a BMW Spyder with a speed of 102.528 mph (164.995 kph).

Here in the west the speedy Miran is completely unknown, as is the top Russian driver Victor Kasankov, who won the last big Formula E race before the Wall came down. The E stands for east.

For years the drivers in the eastern bloc were held to be second–rate amateurs. The West German sports officials saw to this. For journalists the eastern bloc races were absolutely taboo, although many people must have wondered why more than 250,000 spectators went to the Schleiz Triangle races in the fifties. The races couldn't be that bad. In 1961 the West German sports authorities prohibited any participation by West German drivers in Communist sporting events. The athletes on the other hand could still run in the

Home–built Russian racer of 1962. Available knowhow not put into practice

ENTHUSIASM FOR RACING IN THE EASTERN BLOC

Air–cooled 8 cylinder Tatra 603 engine designed prewar by Hans Ledwinka for the advanced streamlined model (left). In standard form the 2,545 cc engine gave 100 bhp, in racing form 170 bhp. A favorite in the eastern bloc

One of the smallest record–breakers ever was built in 1963 in Kharkov. Vladimir Nikitin drove the 12 ft 6 ins (380 cm) long midget down the test course at nearly 186 mph (300 kph)

eastern bloc. It was not until 1972 that the GDR for its part placed a ban on participation by Western European and North American drivers in East German races.

In August 1989 race director Elscher opened the door to the West. He took a big risk and allowed a whole group of West German drivers to compete. Since reunification what were formerly capitalists and socialists coexist happily in the paddock, and provide some very exciting racing. The atmosphere could not be better, since the "old Nürburgring feeling" and all that goes with it is still alive and well here. My Austrian colleague, Dr Krakowizer, even suggested in the local newspaper after attending the race meeting that the Schleiz Triangle races should be put under a preservation order. A challenging idea.

Hartmut, the regular announcer at the circuit, affectionately known to the fans as "the earwig", radiates undiminished optimism about its future, although the German touring car championship has so far omitted the Schleiz Triangle races from its calendar. The prize money expected is too much, and some worries about safety cannot simply be dismissed. Large parts of the circuit are still without safety fencing and run–off areas. The temporary grandstands do not exactly fill the officials from western Germany with confidence. And they have real problems in taking the entrance money: only about one in three even pays the small amount demanded.

But this can all change. At the last race meeting a Munich advertising agency provided the right image with a glossy race program. The most important sponsors unfurled their banners, there was a general hustle and bustle, and a driver from Czechoslovakia admitted to the author with a grin: "Capitalism is fun." ■

INDIANAPOLIS 500: THE MILLION DOLLAR ROULETTE

From down and out to millionaire. The Indy 500 can even be won by a little known driver

The three Indianapolis
races from 1989 to 1991
were won with the
supercharged 2.65 liter
Chevrolet V8 engine,
which produces a healthy
720 bhp at 10,750 rpm.
The designer is the Swiss
Mario Illien. IndyCar
engines only cost a
quarter of the amount
needed for a Formula 1
Ferrari or Honda engine,
but the output is
identical. Aerodynamics
are more important than
power

BOSCH

PPG
CART

MEARS

1987
USAC

PENNZ

Rick Mears (right) has already won four Indianapolis 500s for the Penske team. His toughest rival is Michael Andretti (below). Both earn a good 10 million dollars a year in the CART series (in the USA the incomes are published). The Penske–Chevrolet can reach just under 250 mph (400 kph), 25 mph (40 kph) faster than a Formula 1 racer. Over 100 racing cars turn up in the hope of qualifying as one of the 33 fastest. Practice lasts for 21 days!

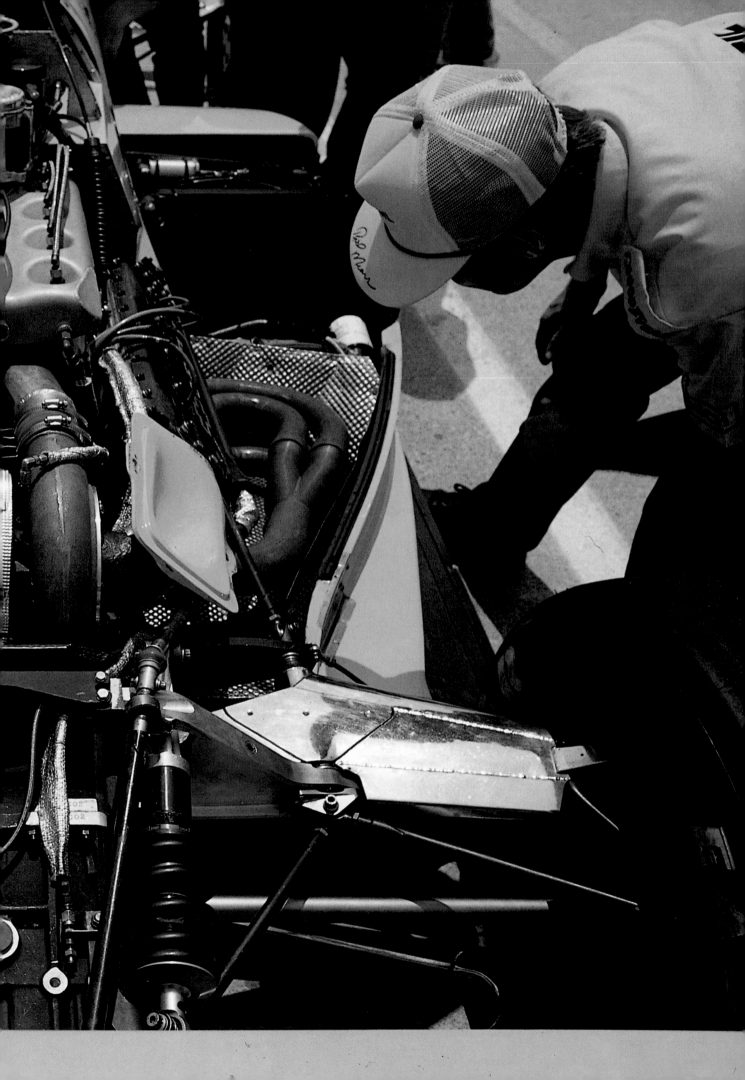

Compared with Formula 1 designs, IndyCar racers are built on simpler lines and are easier to maintain. This reduces costs and attracts more teams and sponsors. Lola and March supply most of the teams with their carbon fiber chassis. The Penske team now uses their own design of chassis with aerodynamic refinements

ALL THE DRAMA OF THE 500 MILE RACE: 440,000 AMERICANS ARE THERE TO WATCH

Even previous no–hopers can win the 500 Mile Race. Here the former Tyrrell driver Danny Sullivan, who had little success in Formula 1, is celebrating a magnificent victory in the 1985 race. Winnings: well over a million dollars for a bare three hours' work. In 1991 Mark Dismore (above) rams the crash barrier at an acute angle on one of the straightaways, traveling at over 230 mph (370 kph). The carbon fiber chassis does not give way, and Dismore's injuries are only slight. Nothing short of a miracle

Barely 30 miles (48 km) from the finish the Penske driver Rick Mears prepares to overtake the leader Michael Andretti on the outside of a bend at about 230 mph (370 kph). The commentator screams into the microphone, quite beside himself: "Rick is going into the wall!" But all goes well. By daring to do the apparently impossible, Rick Mears in 1991 again won the most famous race in the world, the Indianapolis 500 Miles Race. His unique record is 14 starts, 4 victories and a cool 1.8 million dollars in the bank. Rick was for many years the best man in the legendary stable of Roger Penske, who deserves the title of "Mr Indianapolis."

"I'm not interested in second place, my car has to win." These were Roger Penske's words on his first visit to Europe over 20 years ago. The journalists knew what they were listening to: a typical bigmouth with nothing to back up his words. In those days nobody in Europe had heard of Mr Penske from faraway California. Porsche's development chief Helmut Bott was told by an American photographer: "Mr Penske drives in sports car races himself and earns his money with a Chevrolet agency. His stock car racing team is doing well. His men stand out because of their clean overalls, really smart boys."

What Mr Penske said to Porsche racing boss Helmut Bott after visiting the pits seemed to us pro–German and therefore pro–Porsche journalists a terrible blasphemy: "It's basically good, but the finish leaves something to be desired." He was referring to the 700 bhp Porsche 917 sports racer with its 5 liters and 12 air–cooled cylinders. THE supercar, even seen from today's viewpoint. Porsche's top technical boss looked the American straight in the eye and

121

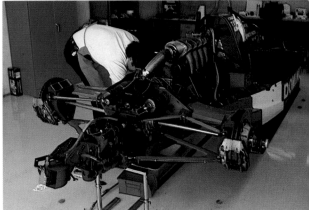

RACERS ON METHANOL: THE LAP RECORD IS JUST ON 230 MPH (370 KPH)

Indianapolis is a law unto itself. The driver who wins is often not the fastest in absolute terms. What is needed is perfect physical fitness coupled with the right feel for the technology involved, and a good dash of cleverness. The 59-year-old gentleman in the white overalls is A.J. Foyt, who has already won the 500 Mile Race four times

said drily: "It's good enough to beat the Ferraris." End of conversation. In those days one didn't want to have anything to do with people like that. Six months later Penske's blue Sunoco Ferrari 512 beat all the works cars and the whole Porsche team. Penske's meticulous preparation paid off. At Porsche his organizational talent was recognized, and they let him have the latest Porsche sports racers. But his mechanics dismantled the cars down to the last nut and bolt. The Penske team then had one victory after another in the CanAm series. It began to get boring. The first Indianapolis win for his McLaren driven by Mark Donohoe against 32 Eagles in 1972 opened the door for the success of his business. It was the breakthrough for an unparalleled career – from a small–time racing team owner to a multi–millionaire with at present more than 11,000 employees and a good three billion dollars in annual turnover. He is now majority shareholder in the world's largest truck hire and leasing company, Hertz Rent a Truck, with a fleet of 60,000 trucks. The highly reputed Detroit Diesel Engine Works have been his property since 1989. His Toyota dealership sells about 26,000 cars per year. One irony is that Penske now has about 3,000 more employees on his payroll than Porsche, and has considerably higher turnover and profit figures.

Because he did not find the Ford Cosworth engines all they might be, he had the "unbeatable" Chevrolet V8 IndyCar engine designed by the British Ilmor racing engine firm owned by the Swiss designer Mario Illien. Penske's shareholding in the firm ensures that it is he who decides in the last resort which other team gets the latest engines. ■

Bobby Rahal last won the 500 Mile Race in 1986 (top picture). In 1972 and 1974 Emerson Fittipaldi became Formula 1 world champion, but it was not until 1989 that he had his first win in the Indianapolis 500 (big picture). Supreme: America's biggest oval seen from the air (left).

A 4,000 HORSEPOWER KICK – DRAGSTERS ON THE LIMIT

This is no misprint. The fastest dragsters can accelerate from a standing start to 312 mph (502 kph) in 4.95 seconds

Don Garlits unleashes all those horses. He has been thrilling his fans for over 25 years more than any other racing pro. Don was the initiator of the incredibly long Top Fuel dragsters. Starting with a puny 300 bhp in 1951, the year that dragster racing was born, the power available rose continuously to an awesome 4,000 bhp by the beginning of 1992. The starting point is still the same: a V8 engine with some exotic internals astride which is a huge supercharger

A "Funny Car" before the start. The sponsors insist on the seemingly standard bodywork. There is little difference in the engine department between the Top Fuel contenders and the highly tuned Funny Cars. However a Funny Car with up to 4,000 bhp is not easy to drive. The shorter wheelbase makes it more difficult to stay in lane when accelerating. Top speed: nearly 300 mph after 5.2 seconds. The supercharged 8 cylinder engine is in front of the driver

The National Hot Rod Association is the umbrella organization for drag racing in America. It finds the prize money from advertising revenue, which in 1992 totaled 12 million dollars. The television rights are on top of this. With all this money it is possible to pay for such star attractions as this 330 mph 16,000 horsepower jet–propelled dragster, which is here seen lighting its afterburner. The finals always take place at night – this makes it more exciting

The duel between two Top Fuel dragsters is only decided over the last few yards because the full power output of 4,000 bhp cannot be put down onto the road over the full distance. The tires can take about 2,500 bhp at the start, and after about 150 yards a Top Fuel dragster has sufficient directional stability for the driver to use full power. The first second of the race usually decides who wins. Jubilation: daddy won again (inset)

FAST MOUSE WITH 2,000 BHP: SHIFTING INTO FOURTH SPEED AT 186 MPH (300 KPH)

Nostalgia dragsters are the latest fad for the Californian speedway freaks. The gray Fiat Topolino (or "Mouse") with the supercharged 2,000 bhp V8 engine is basically 35 years old. Back in those days the speed merchants put their faith in two 7.5 liter V8 engines (center). The yellow hot rod (above) has 850 bhp under the hood and is converted at weekends into a modified dragster capable of 193 mph (310 kph)

Just forget everything you have ever learned in the way of acceleration figures for racing cars. Nothing can touch the fastest dragsters. Incredible feats are achieved on the quarter mile (402 m) long dragstrip. The noise from the two roaring supercharged engines easily exceeds that achieved by a whole pack of 32 Formula 1 racers. The road surface trembles under your feet if you go within 10 feet (3 m) of the dragsters.

Photographers only make this mistake once, because after this you are deaf, even wearing the obligatory ear protectors.

It's no use trying to run away, as your shoe soles will be glued to the asphalt. The glue is made up of sizzling hot tire rubber, an explosive cocktail of nitromethanol and gasoline, and molten tar. These are left from the "burnout" or prestart. Anyone with weak nerves would be bound to pass out if not in the safety of the stands more than 50 yards (or meters) away when a pair of Top Fuel dragsters leave the start. In the final round for the American championship the competition is really fierce for everyone, even so this is the fairest form of motor sport anywhere. In the man–to–man struggle there is only a winner and a loser. The bare statistics of the best times of the day speak for themselves: Barry Ormsby covered the quarter mile in his Top Fuel dragster in 4.897 seconds. The average speed was precisely 302.708 mph (487.14 kph) with a finishing speed of well over 310 mph (500 kph) – but this does not count for victory. What decides it is the fastest time from start to finish. Ayrton Senna's 750 bhp McLaren–Honda Formula 1 racing car accelerates to 100 mph (160 kph) in just under five seconds. The Brazilian also has to make six gear shifts in reaching his top speed of

RICO ANTHES' DRAGSTER IS THE FASTEST MERCEDES

For years Germany was simply not on the dragster map. Today more than 50,000 spectators make the trip to Hockenheim to see Germany's fastest driver, Rico Anthes, in action. His beautiful Mercedes Funny Car coupe is a popular attraction even at American events. Rico's supercharged 8300 cc V8 engine (above left) is a mouthwatering sight for the connoisseur. The blonde Sylvia Anthes (above right) keeps her foot down to embarrassingly good effect in her Willys coupe as far as the male competition is concerned

230 mph (370 kph). Dragsters only have a single "gear". The fastest dragsters are fitted with a planetary transmission, which relays the power of the engine to the rear wheels without any snatches. Just a couple of years ago two–speed transmissions were considered adequate. Today the power of the engines far exceeds the ability of the tires to put it down on the road, in spite of the compulsory prestart or "burnout" in which the tires are brought up to the optimum temperature. With 4,000 bhp being transmitted, the wheels even with up to 3 foot (1 m) wide tires spin so fiercely from the start to the halfway point that any correction would inevitably lead to a collision with the crash barriers. The secret for putting up the very best times does not therefore lie in maximum engine performance, since all the top teams have the same technical starting point. The driver can only solve the problem of too much horsepower with the aid of the on–board computer, which shows in addition to engine data the acceleration figures on a continuous basis. In practice it is the first second which decides which will be the best time at the finish. Because no tire can put down 4,000 bhp onto the asphalt without spinning, the driver only utilizes about 2,000 bhp in the first second. The electronic engine management system only permits the preset amount of power to be used at the start. After the first two tenths of a second the driver determines by means of throttle pedal pressure how much horsepower he needs to maintain a balance between maximum acceleration and tire adhesion. Keeping the car in a straight line can become a real problem. Including the driver, a race–ready Top Fuel dragster only weighs about 1,870 pounds (850 kg). With 4,000 bhp on tap, this means a power to weight ratio of about 5,000 bhp per ton. The most powerful Formula 1

90 PERCENT NITROMETHANOL
PROVIDES THE PUNCH

cars have a power to weight ratio of less than 950 bhp per ton. If all of the dragster's 4,000 bhp could be put down onto the road from the start, it should be able to accelerate four times as fast as the Formula 1 racer, given the same aerodynamics.

Nowadays the aerodynamics can only be worked out with the aid of a computer. In the case of Rico Anthes' first Mercedes Funny Car dragster the whole body was bent by the wind pressure which kept increasing at an ever faster rate. This changed the handling to such an extent that Europe's fastest Funny Car driver only prevented the car from rolling over sideways at 224 mph (360 kph) by making instant corrections with the steering, the Funny Car jumping from one rear wheel to the other as he did so. Consequently the likable Frankfurter had a new dragster built in Texas, which is known as "Rico's Benz" and provides plenty of sound and fury on the dragstrips of Europe.

The fastest European dragsters are only fractions of a second slower than the most outstanding American machines, since all the internals of the V8 engines without exception also come from Detroit.

The weekly magazine "National Dragster" in the USA shows just how tough this business of the quarter mile dash is. 34 drivers are listed in the Top Fuel/Funny Car class whose times come within two tenths of a second of one another. Nigel Mansell won his fourth Grand Prix in succession in 1992 by all of 34 seconds. It is admittedly difficult to compare a Grand Prix racing car with a dragster, but a little more careful control of the throttle foot at the start would help many a Formula 1 driver to achieve better results.

The drivers do not always have the luxury of a 540 yard (500 m) braking area. So Rico Anthes' 230 mph (370 kph) Funny Car is here seen shooting past the course markers with red hot brakes and ballooning brake parachute. Careful preparation for the start is vital for survival (top left). The fastest European dragsters were bought from the States (top right)

THE OUTLAWS: 800 BHP AND NO BRAKES

The last front–engined giants in the history of the automobile are 100 bhp more powerful than Grand Prix racers

The American Outlaw racers achieve incredible speeds on their half–mile (804 m) oval speedway tracks. Because they always circulate anticlockwise, the two half–axles are of different lengths. The wheel camber is also different for the two sides. Most drivers make do with a starting gear and a high gear, but planetary transmissions with direct drive are permitted and are catching on in spite of the higher cost. An 800 bhp Go Kart!

The wingless sprintcars are the kings of the sand tracks. All the famous Indianapolis stars come from the sprintcar scene. What is needed is the ability to control 800 bhp in the tight confines of a pack of 33 cars. The winners of the heats start right at the back in the final and so they have to drift their way right through the field to get to the front. A ruthless way of sorting the men from the boys

DRIFTING INSTEAD OF BRAKING. TAKE YOUR FOOT OFF THE THROTTLE AND YOU'VE LOST

Racing on ovals places extremely high stresses on the driver. The head and its crash helmet are such a strain for the neck muscles that many drivers without headrests have passed out. Since 1990 an anchoring harness for the crash helmet and a neck support have been compulsory. The padding on the bodyframe does something to cushion the shocks from the track surface. Rolling over several times is quite common in sprint races; the spectators like this, but the drivers would rather do without it

Almost every American boy wants to be a race driver one day. The Indy 500 is the dream, but the bumpy oval track by the freeway exit is the reality. It is here that fathers and sons live out their dreams of being the amateur driver who leaves his famous rivals trailing. The leap to competing at Indianapolis is then only a question of time.

In fact these dreams can be realized. Every American Indianapolis driver has to be able to show proof of wins on the ovals with a front–engined racer before he can take the rookie test. In the rookie test which precedes the actual qualifying practice sessions the driver has to complete five consistently fast laps. There must not be a time difference of more than ten per cent between the second and fifth laps. This aptitude test is very important because the drivers whose speed constantly varies hold up the race. For the rookie test there is therefore only one driver on the track at a time.

After the rookie test comes the actual qualifying. About 70 drivers with 110 different cars apply for the 33 places on the grid. In Grand Prix races a maximum of seven drivers fail to qualify in their practice session, and cannot start in the race. But the number of good performers in the US front–engined racing scene is so high because everyone is familiar with the regulations and in North America alone there are more than 2,000 speedway tracks. The races are every Friday and Saturday evening.

The continuing love affair with the front–engined racing car has a historical reason. For many years some of the fastest Indy racers were built in tiny workshops. Two rigid axles, a powerful engine and plenty of spunk were enough to get you a good place in the Indy 500 right up into the

■ OVAL RACERS ARE IN ACTION EVERY WEEKEND

Every town of any size in the USA has a speedway oval. Instead of going to the cinema, the whole family goes to the sprintcar racing. The charm of this low–cost form of racing is that the cars are all on absolutely level terms. Almost any stock V8 of over 5 liters is *converted into a racing engine. Sophisticated goodies are expressly forbidden. Repairs have to be made with basic welding equipment. Consequently an 800 bhp sprintcar ready to race can be had for a mere 30,000 dollars*

THREE–WAY CATS ARE COMPULSORY FOR OVAL RACING

Tubular space frames are a must for all oval racers. Every team takes two frames along to the race meeting, long or short depending on the course. Fuel injection or carburettors, anything goes, as long as there is no supercharging or turbocharging. Nitrous oxide injection is permitted in Texas on Outlaws. The racing tires are recycled examples with handcut treads

sixties. The local scrapyard provided the parts for most of the drivers. The turning point came with increasing technical sophistication.

In May 1964 420,000 spectators witnessed the last victory by a front–engined racer in the Indianapolis 500 Miles Race. The legendary A.J. Foyt in his Sheraton Thompson Roadster for one last time beat the lightweight Lotus–Fords of Jim Clark, Graham Hill and Dan Gurney. The mid–engine principle of Lotus and Cooper proved itself to be superior because of better handling. The following year Jim Clark, Parnelli Jones, Mario Andretti and Al Miller in the mid–engined Lotus–Ford V8s filled the first four places, the best front–engined car being Gordon Johncock's with a four cylinder Offenhauser which finished fifth. Jim Clark set up a new record race average of 154.68 mph (248.92 kph) for the 500 miles (826 kilometers), including pitstops, which were necessary every 30 laps. Johncock was admittedly just 765 yards (700 m) behind in fifth place, so the mid–engined cars only had a narrow advantage. Today's front–engined racers on the ovals are like slightly scaled down Indy racing cars of the sixties.

In those days 430 bhp was the maximum, but today the 8.3 liter 8 cylinder engines give between 680 and 810 bhp. Because they are geared to do only 150 mph in high, the Outlaws have phenomenal acceleration: from 0–62 mph (0–100 kph) in 2.6 seconds. The most important thing to remember is never to drive straight. If you try you will soon get a very abrupt reminder. An 800 bhp oval racer never really goes in a straight line; the car is "balanced" with constant tiny corrections at the steering wheel. It is steered with the throttle pedal. Never was drifting such fun to watch than with these spectacular front–engined projectiles. ∎

WHEN THE WINNER IS A LOSER

In spite of past triumphs, sports car racing is threatened with extinction. The public takes no notice of it

Scrapping wheel to wheel at 220 mph (360 kph); and they are supposedly standard. But the 220 mph stock cars only outwardly resemble the standard product. Because most stock car races are run over 200 to 500 miles (320 to 800 km), quick pitstops are often vital for victory. In the Daytona 500 Miles the drivers change tires 10 times and refuel about 15 times. There is no change of driver. The average age of the drivers in 1991 was 36. In fact it is usually the long–serving veterans on the stock car scene who are leading at the finish. The younger drivers tend to drive their cars too hard

Due to low gearing and four–wheel drive, the highly tuned rallycross racers accelerate faster than today's Formula 1 cars, with up to 700 bhp available. The Audi Quattro S1 (big picture) was built for the Pike's Peak speed hillclimb in Colorado. The Ford RS 200 (left) gives 600 bhp from 2,400 cc, the Austin Metro (designed by the Williams Grand Prix team) 550 bhp. In the center is the unbeatable Peugeot 205 GTI. These continuously developed Group B rally cars would form an interesting basis for a new and more attractive sports car championship

Sheene (right) is in no way inferior to her male rivals. The NASCAR stock cars can be constantly shoved into the car in front thanks to these massive tubular frames and aluminum side panels (below). Here robust V8 engines producing about 600 bhp do the business

WITH A BUDGET OF 150,000 DOLLARS 600,000 CAN BE WON

A handy mechanic easily fits into the engine bay (above left). Fierce scrapping wheel to wheel is not for the faint–hearted. Every lap in the lead counts and increases the prize money. Consequently a driver who drops out just before the finish can also take home a fat wad of prize money. Nets and harnesses with six–point mountings prevent the driver from being thrown out should the car roll over sideways, as frequently happens (above)

7OO husky horses have to be taken seriously. This is where real racing takes off. 700 bhp at the rear wheels means for the driver total concentration for every second of the race. There is no question of taking a breather on the straighter parts of the circuit in these muscle machines. Only a few drivers can stand this constant stress. This is ultimately why the splendid Group B rally cars were abandoned. Outstanding examples of these beasts were the short wheelbase Audi Quattro S1 of Walter Röhrl and the four–wheel drive Peugeot 205. The Group B cars showed up in textbook fashion the inadequate driving skills of some really quite quick drivers. They were unable to use the 700 bhp to best advantage on tricky sections. A number of fatally injured spectators and tragic accidents provided unfortunate proof of this. They led to the abandonment of some important rallies and the banning of the fabulous Group B rally cars.

Rally expert Rauno Aaltonen puts his finger on it: "Overall there are about 75 rally drivers who can handle 250 bhp. At the most 20 drivers can manage 450 bhp, but not even ten works drivers can master 700 bhp under difficult conditions." But in Formula 1 too only a few drivers can keep up the pace over the full distance. Fangio, Stewart, Senna and Prost won their world championship titles because of their unequaled powers of concentration. Today the most powerful rally cars of all time can still be seen in the spectacular rallycross races and the Pike's Peak speed hillclimb in Colorado in the USA. The decline of the sports car world championship cannot simply be attributed to an excess of regulations. The performance of the cars was clearly too much for at least two thirds of the drivers. Hans Stuck, Bernd Schneider and

The 4 cylinder 2,200 cc rallycross engine of the Peugeot 205 (right) in its turbocharged form gives almost exactly as much power as the extremely sophisticated 12 cylinder Mercedes C291 of 3,500 cc

ROCKETING COSTS DROVE THE TEAMS AND SPECTATORS FROM THE RACE TRACKS

Michael Schumacher found themselves pushing back the frontiers of driving experience with their 700 bhp racers into areas unattainable by most amateur drivers. Hans Stuck recorded split times over the twisty inner circuit in the qualifying practice session for the last Daytona 24 hour race with the elderly Porsche 962 that were three seconds faster than those of the victorious Nissan works team. Television transmission times meant all teams made a special effort in practice, as every team wanted to be seen in the lead on the opening laps. The Group C world championship failed not only because of the excessively high costs, but also due to second-rate drivers who made little impression on the press and public. The organizers of the German Touring Car Championship are familiar with this problem. Hence the persistent refusal to admit any type of engine. Mercedes and BMW could otherwise, for instance, fit their new eight and twelve cylinder engines uprated to 700 bhp in a mid position in the Mercedes 190 or BMW M3. With this kind of wolf in sheep's clothing a similar two–class society would be created to that in Group C or Formula 1 today. A handful of top drivers racing for the leading makers would fight it out between them, while the rest bring up the rear.

In the South African and Australian touring car races, cars are allowed to start in the "Super Boss" class which have up to 900 bhp engines in standard bodyshells. They make a splendid spectacle, reminiscent of the American NASCAR stock cars which have enjoyed so many years of success. In years to come these racing production car lookalikes will probably take the place of the Group C sports cars. ■

From a technical point of view, the sports car world championship shot itself in the foot. Costs rocketed with the ban on turbochargers and limit on fuel consumption. Performance comparable to Formula 1 was now required. Mercedes, Jaguar and Porsche gave up

THE DESERT KNOWS NO MERCY

High noon: the Californian desert races are rightly considered a sheer struggle for survival for man and machine

The robust Volkswagen flat four engines are very popular. This Californian offroad racer has a 2.6 liter engine giving a lusty 160 bhp. In racing form the two–seater racer tips the scales at 970 pounds (440 kg). So its attack on this 1 in 3 gradient is correspondingly fast and furious

The uncompromisingly bare bodyshell is all that is left to remind us of the original Beetle. Under the non–existent back seat rumbles a 250 bhp Porsche engine. Long double suspension legs ensure a relatively soft landing after the innumerable leaps several feet into the air. The offroad pros accept the bruises all over their bodies with a shrug. As compared with the motorcycles, four wheels are sheer luxury

THE OFFROAD ACES TAKE ADVANTAGE OF THE END OF THE ARMS RACE

"Have fun in the desert." The fun in the desert has a bitter aftertaste since the tragic events during the Paris–Dakar race. At least 31 drivers and spectators died in the last ten years of the often chaotic offroad event from Paris to Dakar or Cape Town. All one's worst fears were exceeded. Motor racing can be relatively safe as long as organizers and drivers learn from the fatal consequences of previous races. We must remember that in a period of eight years and in more than 150 Grand Prix races there has not been a single fatal accident in Formula 1.

The Californian offroad specialists long ago drew the obvious conclusions from what had happened on the murderous long–distance races. Short, fast offroad courses in the most difficult desert terrain are laid out as circuits. Constant surveillance is therefore guaranteed, and in the case of a breakdown or injury help will soon be at hand.

No organizer can keep a rescue service at concert pitch for several weeks, as would have been necessary in the case of the French races through Africa. Because most organizers have contractual obligations to sponsors and are tied to TV broadcasting times, the conditions under which many a race is run are enough to horrify the safety experts. The main thing, it often seems, is that the race gets reported. But the negative publicity did the French offroad races an enormous amount of harm.

But what happens in the Sahara is of little interest to the American offroad specialists. Europe and Africa are far away, and the American desert areas are even a few degrees hotter than the Sahara. 25,000 Americans regularly compete in more than 300 races which

Triple gas shock absorbers with balancing chambers – a German development by Bilstein which has caught on. Double generators for the night stages. The huge red air filter is changed at each servicing stop. Peace before the storm (above): 200 cars and 150 bikes start in eight classes. Most of the Californian desert races take place on the vast military ranges on the Mexican border

COOPERATION: DRIVERS AND CONSERVATIONISTS WORK TOGETHER

In American desert races the conditions laid down by the conservationists are obeyed to the letter. After the race groups of volunteers collect the rubbish. Every car in the race and all support vehicles have to have catalytic converters. California does in fact have the toughest environmental regulations, even for racing cars. Anyone who throws away a can during the desert race pays a fine of 1,000 dollars. You can only persuade people to behave sensibly by getting at their pockets

are put on every year between Las Vegas and San Diego. Where else can a courageous amateur driver compete successfully against the professionals? Where else is the mixture of adventure, pioneering spirit and sporting contest so thrilling as in this struggle against the heat, the dust and fragile technology?

Most of the races are run nowadays on land previously used for U.S. Army maneuvers. After the race the offroad enthusiasts remove old military junk by the ton and clear the desert of rusty cans and other rubbish. By virtue of this environment–friendly behavior the offroad racing world made a lasting and favorable impression on previously critical conservationists, who had wanted desert races to be banned by law.

What kind of car wins? On the difficult boulder–strewn courses the single–seaters are still the fastest. The most common type of engine is the Volkswagen flat four with turbocharger, giving 200 bhp at the rear wheels from 2,600 cc. Porsche 911 engines give up to 360 bhp, but this much power has to be paid for with increased fuel consumption and chassis problems. Customized Toyota and Nissan pickups with 400 bhp seem to have the best chances at the moment.

Fully automatic or semiautomatic transmissions with up to 12 speeds ensure incredible acceleration even over the steepest sections. Depending on gearing and the character of the course, the fastest pickups can reach a maximum of well over 125 mph (200 kph). Really back–breaking work. "This car kills you," a driver said to me before the start. After 75 miles he really did have to retire – with two broken wrists. As expected, the single–seater won.

WEIGHT SEVEN TONS, MAX 140 MPH (230 KPH)

Any civilized European will soon be choking on his hamburger in horror at the 2,000 horsepower truck show

The Californian pros of the truck racing world compete with correspondingly modified racers either in offroad races or in speedway races, which are being held more and more frequently in roofed over stadiums. This 350 bhp cross–country vehicle is a very successful combination of a stadium and an offroad racer

Attention to detail is the secret for optimum road holding. The setting of the shock absorbers can be adjusted during the race. Thus understeer and oversteer characteristics can be adapted to the nature of the course

The beefy Western truck (left) is pushed further and further toward the outside of the turn by his rival, in order that his excessive speed does not end in a spin. This pushing is perfectly legal, and is a broad hint that the man in front is getting in the way

Showtime in LA's football stadium. 52,000 Monster Truck fans pay 22 dollars each for the 90 minute show. The important thing is to have a roof over one's head, a hot dog in one hand and a coke in the other. The high–speed business of the 90s

TRUCK RACING: A TOUGH TEST FOR THE BIG BRIGADE

The black Dodge (right) was once used to tow mobile homes on the highways. The short chassis is particularly suitable for the speedway tracks. The idea is to have plenty of engine and not much weight. 2,100 bhp from an 18 liter Cummins diesel with turbocharger

RACING TRUCKS HOLD SOME OUTRIGHT COURSE RECORDS IN THE USA

Since the tracks are always left–handed, the chassis is tilted toward the outside of the turns. This makes higher cornering speeds possible. Functional: the instrument panel and the driver (above). The gate money and the money from the sponsors is lumped together and divided fifty–fifty between the drivers and the organizers. A sensible and typically American system for prize money which makes everybody happy

Ever heard of Devil's Bowl Speedway in Texas? There in the remotest corner of Texas, the track is besieged by 120,000 truck fans every Easter. Half a mile (802 meters) long, it is a flat oval with slightly banked turns. The surface varies between slightly bumpy and very bumpy – brown Texan clay, the stuff the native Americans used their huts.

On this weekend any car on the freeway feels like a tiny ant surrounded by an army of beetles: "You stop counting at 10,000 trucks, and they keep on coming." Sheriff Dan Porter calls the whole business "an invasion of totally crazy race fans." but he admits: "The town earns so much money on this one weekend that we gladly agreed to the extension of the half–mile speedway track." Fans on the rampage are unknown because alcohol is strictly forbidden at all American events. The police lock up any beer drinkers without hesitation, and sniff at thermos flasks in case there are any bottles of whiskey hidden inside. For America's truckers the Devil's Bowl Speedway is the hub of the universe.

Naturally the fans need no persuading to come and see the souped up trucks. Fierce scrapping for position is guaranteed, the beefy speedsters are a fantastic sight, and direct contact with the drivers before and after the race gives a feeling of belonging, which is what every true racing enthusiast wants.

In the States all nine leading truck manufacturers take part in the twelve big races for the Great American Truck Racing Championship (GATR). These are Ford, General Motors, Kenworth, Mack, Western Star, International, Dodge, and Freightliner Daimler–Benz, as well as White Volvo. The three most important engine manufacturers (Cummins, Mack and Detroit

185

LATE BRAKING: PASSING ONE'S RIVAL AT 118 MPH (190 KPH)

New types of racing are mushrooming everywhere which are in stark contrast to the classical form practiced by the motor racing establishment. The Truck Grand Prix at the Nürburgring, for instance, is an extremely well attended event with over 120,000 spectators, which gives good value for money. Top driver is Bernd Glöver (above) with his yellow Phoenix M.A.N. truck. Bickel Tuning enter this 1,400 bhp product of their own workshops to compete against the works drivers of Mercedes, Scania, Volvo, and other famous makes. Success is encouraging

Diesel) support the teams with special parts and 400,000 dollars prize money. The grand total of prize money comes to about three million dollars and is shared fifty–fifty between the organizers and the teams. Technically the American speedway racing trucks are slightly scaled down production vehicles. In the case of European racing trucks the chassis measurements have to be identical to those of production models. There are no restrictions on the choice of engine in America, as long as diesel engines are used. Also the number of cylinders and the position of the engine are of no consequence in the States, another contrast with the rules for European racing trucks. The performance in terms of sheer power is of relatively little importance on the sandy speedway circuits; the wheels always spin in any case. The output varies between 1,800 and 3,200 bhp. The brakes are also of little importance, since going sideways in the turns provides the braking effect.

European racing trucks are fitted with water–cooled disc brakes, giving braking figures better than many a 140 mph (230 kph) prestige car. For safety reasons these racing trucks also have a governor restricting maximum speed; 100 mph (160 kph) is the limit. The American organizers take a more lenient view and do not require any such devices. At the Pocono Raceway in California the winner's terminal velocity was exactly 143.72 mph (231.28 kph). This drew the following remark from course commentator Joe Mattioli, made to a reporter: "The idea of a 13,000 pound truck going at 140 mph – if that doesn't capture your imagination, you'd better pinch yourself – you're probably dead." He's got something there.

400 MPH (650 KPH) WITHOUT FEAR

The lonely driver on the salt lake needs three things: bags of power, safe tires, and plenty of courage

The fastest of them all: Stan Barrett took his 60,000 bhp rocket–powered Budweiser three–wheeler through the sound barrier. Bill Fredrick (right) worked for 7 years on this audacious project. The cramped cockpit gave its driver claustrophobia (far right). Barrett exceeded 620 mph (1,000 kph) 21 times. He succeeded in breaking through the sound barrier in December 1979 with a speed of 739.542 mph (1190.122 kph) on the space shuttle runway at Edwards Air Base

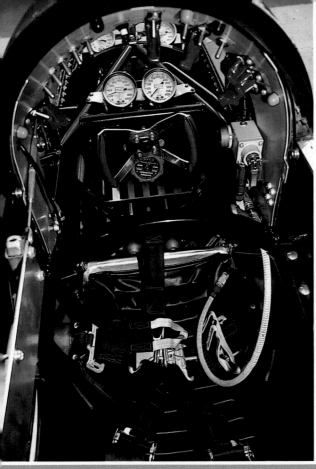

INDEX OF THE CARS ILLUSTRATED

ACKNOWLEDGMENTS

Transedition Books would like to thank the following: Maria Feifel of Daimler–Benz AG for her patience in seeking out previously unpublished racing material; colleagues at Ferrari for insights into the history of the firm; the historical archive of the Indianapolis Raceway; Arthur Westrup and Beate Zartmann for information on the victorious NSUs; the Museum for Historic and Aerodynamic Vehicles in Mögglingen for permission to photograph some rare racing cars; Ulrich Schwab and Reinhard Lintelmann for some of the best photographs from their collections.
Photographs: all the photographs were taken by Hans G. Isenberg with the exception of the following: autopress, Neckarsulm p.28; Daimler–Benz AG, Stuttgart pp. 3–6, 18–20, 28–33, 46, 53–55, 104, 158–159; Ferdi Kräling, Winterberg title page; Reinhard Lintelmann, Espelkamp pp. 24–25, 28–29, 37, 40–41, 46–47, 49, 56–57; Ulrich Schwab, Stuttgart pp. 12–16, 50–51, 56–59, 62, 63–67, 72–77, 80–85, 88–89, 92–93, 99; Thill/ATP back cover.

German language text and photographs
© Falken Verlag GmbH 1992
English language edition
© Transedition Books 1994 a division of Andromeda Oxford Limited, 11–15 The Vineyard, Abingdon, Oxon OX14 3PX

Translation: Robin Sawers

Printed in Spain in 1994

Published in Germany in 1992 by Falken–Verlag GmbH, Niedernhausen/Ts.

This edition published in the USA in 1994 by Chartwell Books, Inc., a Division of Book Sales, Inc., Raritan Center, 114 Northfield Avenue Edison, NJ 08818

ISBN 0-7858-0138-3